This

War Is the
PASSION

This War Is the PASSION

Caryll Houselander
Author of *The Reed of God*

Christian Classics ⟡ Notre Dame, Indiana

© 2008 by Ave Maria Press, Inc.

Founded in 1865, Ave Maria Press is a ministry of the Indiana Province of Holy Cross.

www.christian-classics.com

ISBN-10 0-87061-245-X   ISBN-13 978-0-87061-245-9

Cover and text design by John Carson.

Printed and bound in the United States of America.

Library of Congress Cataloging-in-Publication Data
Houselander, Caryll.
  This war is the passion / Caryll Houselander.
    p. cm.
  Originally published: New York : Sheed & Ward, 1941.
  ISBN-13: 978-0-87061-245-9
  ISBN-10: 0-87061-245-X
  1. War--Religious aspects--Catholic Church. I. Title.

BX1795.W37H68 2008
264.8'73--dc22
                        2007046688

CONTENTS

FOREWORD

"And I, when I am lifted up from the earth, will draw all people to myself."

(John 12:32)

The text from John's gospel, cited above, could almost stand as a shorthand description of how Frances Caryll Houselander (1901–1954) understood the meaning of Jesus Christ: the one who, lifted up on the cross, not only draws all to himself but binds together all in his mystical body of which he is the head.

This War Is the Passion, published in 1941, was Caryll Houselander's first book. It became, unexpectedly, a best-seller both in Houselander's native England and in the United States. Originally a series of articles published in the *Grail* Magazine, the writer and Catholic publisher, Maisie Ward (who would later write Houselander's biography) ran across those articles and encouraged her to make them into a book. Houselander wrote during Britain's precarious days in its war with the axis powers of Germany. The book is redolent of those siege circumstances suffered, beginning in 1939, by the British people: rationing, dislocations of populations, the constant fear of bombing, shortages of everything from decent food to medicines, mobilization of the young, transferals of young children outside of London to the countryside and so on.

The particular angle of her book was this: how does one see the terrors of war through the lens of Jesus Christ? Notice that I said "Jesus Christ" and not something abstract like "faith" because Houselander was a visionary believer in Christ who saw everything through the nourishment she found in the Gospels and the strength of her intense life of prayer centered on the liturgy. In fact, she numbered among the discomforts of life during war the difficulty of getting to daily Mass.

Houselander's life could not be justly described as a happy one. Born in 1901, her parents divorced, and she was raised by a mother who could only charitably be called "difficult." Raised as a Catholic after the conversion of her mother, she broke with the church in her adolescent years only to recover her faith, not through some intellectual path, but through three intense visionary experiences of Christ himself. The most famous of these revelatory epiphanies was a luminous living experience of Christ in every person surrounding her while she was traveling on the London underground. That experience convinced her that Christ was to be found in every person and not in the saints alone. It is almost as if she intuited the doctrinal underpinnings of the mystical body of Christ by sheer personal experience.

Her life in the 1920s was a critical one; she had returned to the practice of her faith in 1925, but in the same decade she had a passionate love affair with the famous British spy Sidney Riley (the inspiration for the fictional character James Bond) who abruptly broke off the relationship to marry another woman. Houselander herself was never to marry, and the breakup itself was a shattering event in her life.

She did not start out as a writer but as a skilled illustrator, wood carver, and designer, contributing mainly to popular Catholic magazines. *This War Is the Passion* marked the breakthrough for her becoming a notable writer, and from its publication until her painful death from breast cancer in 1954, she published a whole series of books that made her one of the more well-known figures in the pantheon of Catholic spiritual writers before Vatican II. In the post Vatican II period, her reputation all but disappeared, and it has only been in the past few years that she has been rediscovered and appreciated.

Like many first books, this one points in two quite different directions: one back to her earlier religious experiences and the other as an indicator of what would be the subject of books that would fill out her ideas only casually mentioned in this work. Since her life was largely shaped by her sense of Christ's presence, that sense gives shape to her book as a whole. Her plea was a simple one: The exigencies brought about by war allow everyone to cross the borders of class and occupation, giving people the opportunity to pitch in as helpers of national service. However, such work is also a moment to make Christ real. If one, for example, volunteers at a hospital it is crucial, she writes, not to think of wards full of "cancers" but "Christs." Again, she notes that the poor are often forgotten in the demands of defense. But, she writes, "If we forget our poor now we might as well surrender at once to those who tread the Christ-bloom of the world into the mud."

This lens, which is Christ, is the constant in the way Houselander "sees" in this work. At the same time, some of her foundational themes about Christ here would receive further attention in later work. One example: There is a wonderful meditation on the Way of the Cross in this book—a favorite subject to which she would return later in her life with the posthumous publication of the illustrated *The Stations of the Cross* (1955) with her beautiful wood engravings and her *The Way of the Cross* (1955).

The open sympathy she had for others, the vivid sense of Christ living in all people, was not simply literary adornment. She worked as a counselor and therapist (despite a total lack of formal training) for those children emotionally shattered by trauma and loss; a task she continued even after the war. The explanation of her success in these endeavors, a well-known psychologist remarked, was that she loved them into health. Her approach has been well described as a contemplative entering into the passion of Christ through compassion.

A recent commentator on Houselander's life and work has said that Maisie Wards' admiring biography of Houselander was flawed both because of her prudish inability to deal with her affair with Sidney Riley and, more importantly, because she pictured Houselander in far too solemn a fashion.[1] She managed to turn Houselander into a dour and solitary ascetic. In reality, Houselander was a chain smoker who would not turn down a pint in a pub. She disliked organized forms of Catholic piety, which explains why she broke with the Grail Movement with which she had early been associated. She had little use for the pacifism of the Catholic Workers. She was suspicious of all lay associations out of worry for their tendency to codify the spiritual life into "rules." She had a particular loathing for hothouse piety. In a pungent comment she once said that every Christian had an obligation "not merely to exist, not merely to pickle himself in piety like a gherkin in vinegar to be opened awaiting the Eternal Feast.... He must live, that is to say, to see himself as a part of the whole." In the same spirit she insisted that "Catholicism is something infinitely more than a vast penitentiary; it is the source of all the wonder and poetry and beauty of life and its feasts glorify God as much as its fasts."[2]

One does not see much of that lightheartedness in this work. She writes out of urgency triggered by war. She interweaves meditations on the Gospel of Christ as well as an insistence on practical things her readers might do, not to advance the "war effort," but to become more conformed to Christ. The conditions of war are the occasion for a particular response in Christ. What one does not find in this book is "theory" either about life or the spiritual life; she has an instinctive resistance to such matters. In fact, she addresses such "experts" directly with her own approach to such theory. On the opening page of the second chapter of this book, she writes: "I speak to the virtuosa of the spiritual life, to the expert in spirituality with her networks and hieroglyphics and all the rest. Don't be an expert on the spiritual life. Treat Christ as the real Person that he is, don't fuss and worry about your soul."

More than once Houselander will invoke the "poetry" inherent in Christ. As an artist herself, she understands that art is a form of making (*poesis*) and that making breaks out in beauty. While her writing is not affected, it does in places break out into urgent poetry directed to Christ. Almost always this poetry links Christ to everyone in the world—the "hidden" (mystical) Christ. A small example might suffice: "So it is that Christ is in us, acting and yet resting, his hands lifted and yet toiling, nailed to the cross and yet healing. His feet are nailed to the cross above life's flowering meadows, and yet they are walking the common streets of all the cities in the world, the Shepherd's feet following his wandering sheep."

This first book of Houselander, one would hope, might tempt the reader to read others, thus contributing to a new flowering of interest in this passionate artist and spiritual writer. Many of her books are enhanced with her own works of art; the woodcuts remind many of the work of Eric Gill. She was once called a "divine eccentric"—a sobriquet that became the subtitle of the Maisie Ward biography. That she had her eccentricities is clear but, unlike, say, her contemporary Simone Weil, she was far from a tragic figure. It would be closer to the mark to say that she was a paradoxical one. Frances Caryll Houselander was an obscure working artist who became a well-known author; a solitary figure who was passionate about the community of all in Christ; a worker with her hands who became a therapist via her heart; one who loved the church as community but resisted communities within that community.

May many readers be drawn to the thought and prayers of this unjustly forgotten, once celebrated member of the Catholic Literary Revival. In reaction to her death on October 12, 1954, another member of that august literary group, Monsignor Ronald Knox, wrote that "she seemed to see everyday for the first time, and the driest of doctrinal considerations shone out like a restored picture when she had finished with it." Exactly.

Lawrence S. Cunningham
The University of Notre Dame

1. Wendy Wright. *Caryll Houselander: Essential Writings* (Maryknoll, NY: Orbis, 2005). This is an excellent introduction to Houselander's life and work.
2. Ibid.

ONE

THIS WAR IS THE PASSION

For us, the war is the passion of Christ. There is no need now to dwell on its cruelty. We shall not be able to forget that. To the natural eye it seems that out of this war nothing could possibly result but bitterness, hatred and ruin; and indeed, nothing else could result from it were it not for one person—Jesus Christ, our Lord.

Because he has made us "other Christs," because his life continues in each one of us, there is nothing that any one of us can suffer which is not the passion he suffered. Our redemption, although it was achieved completely by our Lord, does, by a special loving mercy of his, go on in us. It is one unbroken act which goes on in the mystical body of Christ on earth, which we are.

These things are mysterious, we can't understand them with our brains, but now everyone is going to learn to understand them in sorrow, in courage, and in sacrifice. Now the time has come for each of us to prove our Christhood.

Not one of us is alone. All are one in Christ, and we can be strong in the realization that we are together and that we share in all and every grace of one another. We are one, not only with each other, but with all the Church, the saints in heaven, the faithful on earth and the souls in purgatory, and we have, all of us, the strength of our adored King, Christ, as our sword: his strength and his meekness, his love and his forgiveness.

Some of us, perhaps all of us, will feel sometimes hopelessly alone; certain griefs that we shall know make one utterly alone even in the midst of real friends; certain circumstances which will become fairly general give us the loneliness of homesickness, and events may cut us off from one another physically. But there is not a single thing that any one of us can do which does not affect every other Catholic, which is not, in a mysterious way, his deed too.

The martyrs of Siberia, often without sacraments or Catholic contact for years, have told others of the joy they derived from awareness of their oneness with all other Christians. A certain priest said, in Siberia, before his long martyrdom was consummated in death, "On Saturdays, I was always happy, as so many Catholic children made my confession."

WE MUST MAKE COMPLETE SACRIFICE

We have realized on the natural plane that we can win the war only if we are united; we must be united with one another and with our Allies, and every single one of us must go all out for our single purpose. We must put by all else and be ready to give all we have, to the very last drop of our blood, to bring about our one single purpose. That purpose is to gain and keep freedom.

If such an extreme is our duty to one another as human creatures, how much more is it our duty and our honour to give all we have and are, united in our Christhood, for the kingdom of God. This is not a special war, a sideline, a mere analogy for Catholics; no, freedom *is* the possession of the inward kingdom; and to keep it, and keep it as Christ would keep it, is the heart of the whole war. We are doing the same as all the rest, but because of the unmerited grace of faith, our responsibility is greater, we have to do it with a deeper understanding.

LOVE

I do not hesitate to speak as if it were the last time, and to echo Christ's own final words to his apostles, his last commandment: "Little children, love one another." he said it to his apostles when they were going to be scattered about the world, and each in turn to suffer for him.

This is the first and last vocation of every Christian, to love, and all other vocations are only a shell in which this vocation, to love, is protected. So whatever part each of you plays in the war, it must be done only as a channel through which love is poured. Love alone, love only, can save us from being swamped and swept away by the evil passions that war must let loose—hate, fear, despair.

And love can and will save the world, because this war is Christ's passion in us, and if we dare now to act by faith and to pledge ourselves to let his love be as strong in us as his pain is, then it will bear fruit, in proportion to its magnitude of grief.

Love, and love alone, can make life welcome to us; we can help one another by love, as never before, and nothing else can comfort, encourage, be patient, and heal, as love can do now.

Therefore, we are now at the beginning of the Way of the Cross, with Our Lord leading us; we have to walk in his steps; in this "dry wood" foretold by him, we must have our eyes on the "green wood," on the Christ-Passion in which all things already are new, our first springtide, for which we are again sowing seed, and in this he is our great example of love.

Imitate Christ in His Love

We can imitate him literally. He was mocked and crowned with thorns: He remained silent. If our determination to love our enemy, to include the enemy in our prayer and sacrifice, is at moments beyond us, we can imitate his gentle silence, and go on, go on wearing a crown of thorns in our mind. He welcomed his cross and took it up himself and put it on his shoulder to carry it. We can face the war in his spirit, not glad of suffering for suffering's sake, but glad that, since suffer we must, we can carry our share of the cross as a loving work for each other to help our common redemption. We can think, too, that the load the soldiers carry is the cross, and the same applies to the weight of stretchers, and to all the heavy material loads; they, too, are part of the weight of the one great cross laid on us. We can imitate him by welcoming it, and if it seems too heavy at times we can still turn to him and say: "We praise Thee and bless Thee, O Jesus Christ, because by Thy holy cross Thou hast redeemed the world."

He was stripped naked. We also can be stripped of all we have, and not only of our material goods, but of our ambitions, the closeness of friends, our hope of human joy; in this we can, like Our Lord, prepare for sacrifice.

He was sacrificed on the cross. Some will literally imitate him in his death, and all of us know that when a Christian dies it is Christ Who is dying, and his love has overcome death.

All of us can literally imitate him in the wholeness of sacrifice, in offering all that we are—and that, stripped of our selfishness—to God, as an act of adoration to God and of love for one another.

THE KINGDOM WITHIN

Very soon the shortage of paper will become acute and all the means that we have relied upon, consciously and unconsciously, for so many years to state our faith and offer it to the world, will end—all material means, anyway, telephones, wireless, cars and aeroplanes, printing and so on; all things which Christ never had the use of when he lived on earth and faced the whole world with his tidings of great joy.

What means did Christ have, and what means did he use? He had only himself: his soul and body, his joy and suffering, the infinitesimal amount of work he could get into one limited lifetime, the words he spoke, the hands he used, the prayers he said. He had himself, his life and death, and that is all.

And what means did Christ leave to his apostles when it seemed, as it most certainly did seem, that he was defeated, the cause lost? Did he say: "Clearly this thing can't be done by love, by individuals with only themselves, so I will give them machinery and power, and tremendous success!" No, he gave them just his own divine Spirit, the "Comforter" as he called it. He came, through his spirit, to live in them, and that his presence in them might be ever renewed he gave them his body in the Host and his grace through the sacraments.

He did not choose to live a new, different and more successful kind of life in his apostles, or to avoid a repetition of his violent death; no, all but one were martyred, all were poor and generally alone and persecuted, and none had as much success as a popular preacher on a modern wireless.

Yet, these kept the kingdom; and after them, in age after age, the saints who have walked in their footsteps have done so, and they have done so in only one way, because there is only one way, the way of Christ. "I am the Way, the Truth and the Life."

To-day, we may despair of practically everything, of all the world's traditions, of all material things, of success of any sort as we know it, but there is one thing which is not now endangered, but is on the eve—no, the very morning—of resurrection. That one thing is the only thing that matters: Christ, the life of Christ, in the soul of man.

The fact that we are being put back into the position of the apostles is a safeguard to our faith, because the enemies that assail Christianity are not only the evil forces that are apparent to all, but the subtle temptations that a prosperous world never ceases to propose to individual Christians, the gradual loss of the sharp edge of the uncompromising simplicity of the love of Christ. Now it is clear, our faith will be kept alive as it was kept alive in the days when our forefathers shed their blood on this dear English soil, to hand it on, bright and burning, to us.

They will keep our faith and defend Christ's kingdom who, in the midst of the dangers and in the endurance of the war, keep their own souls alight with the love of Christ. What does it mean? It does not mean preaching and boasting about religion. It certainly does not mean withdrawing from the relentless hard work of everyday life in order to pray. The daily life of one V.A.D. is enough to put to shame the Christian who thinks that way will do.[1]

What it does mean is being one of the many thousands who are actually doing the work, nursing the wounded, working in the factories, digging and sowing the land, working hours and hours of overtime in offices. But doing these things in the name of Christ and with the love of Christ; and while we are at them we will call on him present in us for wisdom, courage and humour to keep us going.

If a chance occurs, we shall explain our faith; at all events we shall be able to. We shall have to know it so well that it is in our blood, and to adhere to it so well that we can in a certain way give it, just by being what we are. Thus we must be the book of the gospels ourselves, with the words and teachings of Christ in our minds, but also in our hearts, and whenever the occasion demands, upon our lips. That is something that the daily Mass reminds us of constantly, when we make the triple Sign of the Cross before the gospel.

We shall have also to be the flowering of Christ, the continuing of his love, and in this way we are like the bread for the Host, sacramental. It may be hard to go to confession, it may be difficult to hear Mass, to receive communion; all those mysteries may be as they were during the Reformation. Then will be the time when we, who have long used the sacrament of penance, taking God's forgiveness over and over again, will ourselves give continual life in the world to this expression of Christ, forgiveness. We will do it by forgiving, by forgiving whatever needs forgiveness, day after day.

We have again and again received him in communion. He has come to us and given us himself in this supreme expression of his love, and now and in the future, if it should become difficult to receive him in the Host, we will ourselves keep this expression of love, communion, alive by giving the Christ in us to whomever we come in contact with by repeated acts of love; by being with them in their fears and reassuring them, by helping them in their poverty by every means we can, by tending their wounds and by nursing them in their sickness.

Thus we return to the primitive Christianity of the apostles, and having, as Christ had, only ourselves, we require no more. All that was false or doubtful will drop off like a dead branch, the wheat will be made white in the fire. It is Christ's passion, and his resurrection is just as certain as it was when he went up to the cross. But his resurrection, like his passion, will not vary from what it was like in his own life. He will not rise in us through force; whichever way the war goes, Christ's rising will not depend on that. He will not rise through legislation, or powerful movements, or brilliant organization, and his rising will not be delayed until there is peace in Europe. He will rise in the humility, the courage and love of those few Christians who will keep his kingdom in their individual souls.

This is our apostolate now, and persisting, clearer than the noise of battle, Christ's words should be heard in each heart: "Fear not, little flock, for it has pleased your Father, who is in heaven, to give you a kingdom.

THE FLOWERING OF CHRIST

If Christ is growing in you, you are growing towards sacrifice. If the spirit of sacrifice is not growing in you, Christ is not growing in you, no matter how ardently you may think of him or how eloquently you may speak of him. But if day after day your life gathers to a culmination of sacrifice, then it is certain that Christ waxes strong in you.

A sacrifice is not, as so many people imagine, a mortification; it is not something that is meritorious according to its degree of unpleasantness; on the contrary, in real sacrifice, there is joy which surpasses all other joys, it is the crescendo and culmination of love.

What is a sacrifice?

A girl of eleven, asked to teach a child of four to "make a sacrifice," taught him to make the Sign of the Cross. Asked why this should be a sacrifice, she answered with supreme wisdom, "Because for a little minute he gives all of himself to God."

For a little minute the child stops jumping and shouting, he stands still, puts his feet together, uses his mind and his hands and his voice for his Sign of the Cross. He is offering himself to give honour to God. It is right, too, that from the very start the idea of sacrifice is connected in the child's mind with the Sign of the Cross, and there is really a resemblance between the child and the God who lives in his soul. For the child is still, his hands, feet, eyes and breath, all are offered to God "for a little minute." And it was thus that Christ was on the cross for three hours, his hands and feet were still, his eyes dim, his last breath praying for us.

The child shuts his eyes with an effort, he screws up his whole face to keep them shut; this is perhaps the hardest part of it, to give up for a few moments the bright and lovely toys that are enchanting him. Christ closed his eyes upon the lilies of the field and the wild birds and all the world that was bright and lovely and dear to him as to no other man.

When we make a sacrifice it is always thus, we have to give something up, not because it is a bad thing—for more often it is a good thing—but the offering of ourselves is a complete offering, it means a whole attention, a whole concentration, a whole donation. In the Old Law God asked for the sacrifice of the first-fruits, the best lamb, the first of all the flocks. He did not accept Cain's sacrifice, because it was not the best. In the New Law he still asks for the first lamb of the flock, the richest fruit of the tree; he asks for Jesus Christ.

Christ was of all men the most perfect, because he was more sensitive, more aware, more in love with the world's loveliness than others. He saw the beauty about him with sharper vision, he valued life more. Again, the world was not only something to make him catch his breath with wonder and love, it was his own, it had for him the added preciousness of being something he had made.

I know someone who owns a carved, Chinese vase. It is a lovely thing of translucent red stone. She never thought very much of it until one day a connoisseur visited her. He just moved the vase to a place where the light shone through it, making it glow with a blood-red warmth, showing the roundness and smoothness of it; and then he stood looking at it, not speaking, except occasionally to murmur, "Thank you."

Christ was more than a connoisseur of all the loveliness of the world; on all of it he closed his eyes to die.

The hands that he stretched out to the nails were strong, capable, craftsman's hands; the body he offered was the body of a young man in the perfection of young maturity; the mind that was then crowned with thorns was the mind of a philosopher and poet, an intellect that could never be equalled.

It seemed, I suppose, a waste. The world so needed men like Christ. Even had he not been God, he would have been among the few who can do so much. He could make men see life in a new way, he gave vision as well as sight, he could make the common life, the workman's life, so splendid, he was such a psychologist, he understood what was in the heart of man—and then he could work miracles!

But for all that, he chose to die, he sacrificed himself. Closing his eyes, he closed them not only on the flowers that were drenched with his blood at the foot of the cross but on the faces of his mother and friends, who looked up at him; in giving himself to God, he gave up everything.

There is a picture painted by Sir William Orpen during the First World War, of a soldier lying dead in a dugout, round him the litter of battle. But the light, the sky, the pools of water, the barbed wire, even the litter and the dead man's cracked boots, are so uncannily beautiful that one has the sense of seeing them with the dead boy's vision, seeing them with the sudden sharp awareness of how beautiful the world is that possesses one when death is imminent. That dead soldier in the picture always reminds me of Christ, he is so essentially a "first-fruit," so young and strong and fitted to live, and the world—his world—given to God is so fair a world.

I say, his world given to God, for it is truly given to God, not merely thrown away. When the four-year-old boy shuts his eyes on his bright toys to make the Sign of the Cross, he is giving them to God, because what he is giving is more than some painted pieces of wood, it is what the toys are to him, his delight in them. And a man who, like Christ, gives up his life for his fellows, gives up to God what life is to him. Hence, the more Christ-like the man, the more perfect the sacrifice; the strong, sensitive, potent man, the man with poetry in his heart and with capable hands, does indeed bring a great offering to be consumed in the fire of love, he brings skies full of stars, mountains and fields and shining waters, he brings all the shining tools and gear and tackle of trade, he brings hours of tenderness that will never be and all the unborn children of his life.

Sometimes it seems very cruel that those who make the great sacrifice are always the finest, that those who escape it deliberately are allowed to enjoy the freedom others' deaths have got for them, to enjoy it at such cost and having given nothing; but the fact is they could give nothing as they have nothing to give. Men forced to battle, going unwillingly as slaves to die, do not make sacrifice. Those who do make a willing sacrifice are redeemers.

REPRISALS?

The war compels us to face problems which we are apt to shelve in times of peace.

One such problem is loving our enemies. To become bitter, to want reprisals, to give way to hatred, is a temptation for many people; it is a temptation that is going to become greater day by day and hour by hour. It is all the more difficult to combat because it is not recognized by everyone as a temptation at all, indeed there is a growing number of people who think it right to hate and that, did we refuse to allow this evil thing to possess us, we could not continue to fight.

Of course, such a view is absolutely un-Christian. Christ's teaching is unmistakable; not only is it forbidden to hate anyone, but we are commanded to love our enemies.

THE CAUSES

One way of combating disease is to find out the causes of it and cure them. This applies equally to spiritual disease; hatred in wartime is something which does really spread like an epidemic disease, and since being free of it is the first condition for even beginning to love, it is well to find out what things are the chief causes of hate and how to cure them.

Probably the most potent of all the causes of hate is *fear.* Fear is an emotion which even in private life can drive people of naturally mild and sweet disposition to commit murder. There is no need to dwell on the causes of the fear affecting us all now. We all know them. We all know how terrible they are, how constant and how real. There is no cowardice in admitting that we are afraid, indeed we should not be human if we were not. But we ought to realize that this fear, unless we face it and learn to understand and even to manage it, will lead to hate.

The second great cause of hate is what I must call *indignant grief.* I think that the people in our big cities who have seen their fellows walking homeless and destitute, refugees in their own country, who have seen the streets they love in ruins, have experienced something of the passion of sorrow Christ knew when he wept over the doom of Jerusalem.

So we have our two great causes of hate, fear and indignation, and they are always with us. We can't forget them; everything, every minute, forces them upon us. What are the remedies?

THE REMEDIES

For fear, love is the only remedy. "Perfect love casts out fear," and even imperfect love, love that struggles to help and hear and grow, can; though it does not wholly cast out fear, reduce it and make it bearable.

Those who suffer most through air raids, or the apprehension of them, are people who think they have nothing to do during them. It is not only members of A.R.P. who can do something to help during raids, it is anyone who puts other people before self.[2] A raid gives the opportunity of countless little acts of love, such as making a cup of tea, lending a pillow or a rug, giving-up the best place, controlling our own feelings in order to help others to be calm and plucky, and when it can be done without irritating, reminding people that they are in the hands of God, or contriving to make them laugh. No sooner do you begin to concentrate on the feelings and needs of people round you than your own feelings and needs become less important and your own fears begin to fade.

If you cannot do anything else for people during raids, you can pray for them. You can remember all the people who will be more afraid than you are, all those whose lives are as precious as yours, and as useful, all those who are in a far, far worse plight than you are, because they are without faith. You can pray for each one by name and so make an act of love.

The indignation and grief caused by the sight of bitter suffering inflicted on innocent people can also be helped by acts of love. But I do not think that this emotion is really hate at all, although it is often mistaken for it; but it can, I believe, turn as easily to love.

Most people now have learnt at least a little about glands and secretions, and know that when someone is suddenly faced with the need for self-defence, adrenalin is poured into their blood; the effect of it is to tone up the whole body and to give the individual a kind of fierceness; they become more tense, warmer, stronger, sometimes even their hair stands on end. Without this adrenalin there would be a great many situations which people could not face up to at all, it is a real necessity. All such mysterious physical reactions are proof of the law of God working in nature.

I see no reason why the same law should not work in the soul. If it does, we could safely assume that the fierce feeling, the intensifying of emotion that indignation rouses in us, is not hate, but a kind of spiritual adrenalin, stimulating and giving us the vigour to face up to things beyond human enduring. It comes to this, the sight of suffering inflicted on innocent people fills us with a kind of violent energy, and that energy can very easily turn to hate, but if we like we can turn it to love instead. And that can be done in the simplest way possible; instead of working ourselves up into a fury and exhausting the extra energy we have got, we can spend it in doing something to relieve the suffering that provoked it.

If ever there was a time when we cannot only take the Sermon on the Mount literally if we want to, but can hardly avoid doing so, that time is now. If we believe that whatever we do to the least of his creatures is done to Christ, then now is the time to give to Christ everything that we are capable of. There are people all round us in need of everything; people who, like him, have literally nowhere to lay their heads, who have no clothes, who have no food. There is not one of the corporal or spiritual works of mercy that is not now crying out to be done, not one that is out of our reach to do. The means, too, are at hand; if we cannot do them by ourselves there are organizations for everything, for receiving and giving clothes and money and food, for finding shelters and homes and rest, and for all the other things that are needed; and these organizations are not affairs of red tape, now that the need is here the response to it has come from human people who are out to spend themselves.

If fear and indignation can generate energy in us which can be turned not to hate of our enemy but to acts of love for those whom he has wounded and robbed, we have already taken a big step towards loving the enemy too. These acts of love, this putting self last, this giving and serving, brace the strain of compassion and tenderness in us. Instead of becoming hard and acid, we shall become gentle and sensitive; instead of inflicting yet another wound on the human race, we shall heal one. If all the energy, the spiritual adrenalin, given to us to face the war, is used up in acts of love, there will be nothing left to hate with, and, moreover, we shall cease to have the capacity for hate.

It is no part of loyalty to hate our enemy, but it is part of our loyalty to help our own countrymen to bear this ordeal, and that can only be done by love in action.

POSITIVE REMEDY

That, however, is still negative, although arrived at by positive means. In finding remedies for fear and indignant grief, and finding that the remedies are acts of love, all we do so far as our enemy is concerned is to reduce our capacity for hate; we still have to learn how to love him.

This is not easy. It calls not only for virile Christianity, but for heroic Christianity. Everything now is on a gigantic scale, evil is so terrific that it almost passes belief, such relentless cruelty, such destruction—what can answer it? Surely not a tepid Christianity, surely not compromise? No, only absolute Christianity, undiluted, heroic, crucified love, which stops at nothing and is ready to give everything, including life itself.

We are faced with terrible odds, and as Christians we hold not simply a code of honour or a great ideal in trust, but incredible though it is, we hold Christ in trust. We have the task of keeping alive in this world the mind and the heart of Christ.

Of course we cannot do it alone. We cannot do it by ourselves. Indeed we have to trust to Christ to do it for us, in us and through us, and our part must be giving ourselves over so wholly to him that he can do it in us.

To begin with, we need to imitate him literally; to ask ourselves at every turn what would he have done, what would he have thought, how would he have felt, what did he say, about this and this and this? What would he have thought about the cruel bombing of civilians, about the drowning of little children? Would he, Who is all justice, all mercy, all tenderness, have loved people who did things like that?

Such things, though dreadful, are not new. As Christ fled, the first refugee, into Egypt, a tyrant seeking to destroy all that Christ stood for murdered a city-full of baby boys. All through Christian history, when people have fought against Christ, against his humility and love, they have always come to a climax of brutality. Christ knew that this would happen. He knew it had happened—what then did he do?

First of all, he hated evil. He hated evil and fought against it. Saint Ignatius thinks of Christ entering his passion as a king, going into battle to fight for the standard of innocence, justice and love, against the standard of evil. That is a true thought. Christ did enter his passion to fight sin, and he thought it worthwhile to give all that he was himself to win that fight.

There has never been anyone who valued life as Christ did. He was himself the source of all life and he told us that he came on earth to give us life and a great increase of life. He was, and of course he knew it, the beauty and splendour and wonder of all the Christian lives that were to come. He was the Man abiding in all men, in a mysterious but true sense; when he took himself to his death he took all Christian men. Knowing what his own life was, he thought it not too great a price to pay to defeat evil. There was for him only one measure against evil, himself: all his loveliness and power and life, and he was God. The price he paid to fight evil was high indeed; the agony in the garden, the betrayal of his friend, the cowardly desertion of nearly all his followers, the utter loneliness with which he faced failure and death, the mockery, the night in prison, the injustice, the crown of thorns, the scourging, the nails, the thirst, the despair, the publicity and the dereliction of his death. None of this was too much for Christ to pay to fight evil, to overcome sin.

Yet, quite equally, it was all done to save sinners; knowing perfectly well that men had caused all the evil he was facing, he suffered it all for their sake, to save them from the only death that could be worse than his, the death of their souls. He died to overcome sin and to save sinners, and his last prayer was that those who had caused him all this might be forgiven, and united to his Father by his suffering. There was no question of blotting out men, of destroying sinners, but only of saving them, of delivering them from the wounds of their own sin.

As Christians we have to copy him literally in this. We believe that what Germany stands for to-day is evil, that it is evil which has become tangible and menacing to the world; we believe that we also as individuals have added something to the awful weight of evil, but that in our enemy it has reached a crescendo and we have got to fight it.

Because this is how we see it, our answer to the challenge of war must be a tremendous "yes"; a "yes" such as Christ uttered to his father in Gethsemane; "yes" to the disillusion, to the discomfort, to the hardship, to the danger and endurance of the war, a "yes," if God asks this of us, to death. And the offering, the "yes," must be not only for our own countrymen but also for our enemy, not only that we may conquer Germany but that we may conquer all humanity, just as love did conquer humanity when Christ died on the cross.

No one can take an active part in the war without taking a risk; in proportion to the sincerity with which anyone tries to do something to help and heal, one takes risks. This is no longer only for soldiers, it is for everyone. The consistent Christian will, with Christ for his strength, be led on to risk all he has, gladly, offering his sacrifice in reparation for all evil. He will see men not as people of different nations at war, but as one great family, wounded, insane, in dire need of healing and help, and in all that he does he will offer the only healing and help there is, Christ in his heart for a sacrifice.

It is a strange procession which leads us from merely not hating to loving our enemy, yet it is one that must lead to that end. But if, imitating our Divine Lord, we can offer the cost of serving our friends equally for them and for our enemies, we shall have solved the problem we set out to solve.

Those who hate are never those who heal. The person who gives his coat, his food, his money, his sleep, his thought, his energy and his life to help others to suffer well is never a hater but always a lover; it is such lovers who will win our peace.

THE GREATER LOVE

Christ, who reiterates all through his gospels "Love your enemies," suddenly, when death comes, says, "Greater love than this no man hath, that he lay down his life for his friends"—suddenly and consolingly he says, not enemies, but friends. Yet there is no contradiction. Christ as man had more enemies than any other man who ever lived; perhaps, tragic though this is, fewer friends, at all events few enough who could stand by him in his passion. his enemies were our enemies too, they were the enemies of all that is Christian for all time. Yet, when he died for them, he had made them his friends. his own power of love and friendship, his own tremendous forgiveness, his own surrender to death, had done it. He had made his enemies his friends.

During the life that led up to his death, Christ lived among his friends; it is true that, like those who should follow him, he had enemies in his own household, it is true that even Peter, who was not his enemy, tried to draw him off from his one inflexible purpose of suffering, it is true that this same human and lovable Peter tried to introduce the idea of revenge, the first and last Christian reprisal was Malachy's ear, and Christ healed it at once. Christ dealt with sickness, weakness, fear and wounds all through his public life. He lived with the homeless, he was one of them. His compassion, as a man, was sharpened and increased by the contact with all kinds of grief, by serving all kinds of men and women and helping them to suffer.

Along with this, his condemnation of evil, his open hatred of it, never for a moment failed. Indeed it was precisely this which brought him to his early death. But, as he looked at the world from the cross and saw those sinners who had brought evil into the world, and not only those of his own day but of our day, he saw them as people themselves wounded by evil, twisted out of shape, mutilated, too much hurt to be able to put themselves right. The love so readily and abundantly responsive through continual use among his friends flowed out to these sinners; the same love, the love that compelled men, even unconsciously, to be his friends. So, he died for them.

We are in the world now as Christs; in the midst of this storm. We are here to keep Christianity alive, to keep Christianity pure, intact, to ensure by our own lives in Christ that the gates of hell shall not prevail against Christendom. This cannot be done if there is the least compromise with love; if we do not try to cast out fear by loving acts, if we do not use the energy grief gives us in loving acts, if we do not imitate Christ literally, we shall succumb to hate or to despair.

Our war work, then, is difficult. It is just the work that Christ himself feared in Gethsemane, and yet faced and accomplished, and will accomplish in each of us.

It demands from us wisdom to see clearly and to keep our balance, and to discipline and order our lives to that end, but it demands also blind faith. All his "hard sayings" must be accepted literally; we must obey him absolutely, trust him absolutely, and for his sake love absolutely. With this attitude we can work and hope for peace, for oneness of all human creatures, for the promised blessedness, when "God shall wipe away all tears from their eyes, and death shall be no more. Nor mourning, nor crying, nor sorrow shall be any more. For the former things are passed away."

---

1. V.A.D. stands for "Voluntary Aid Detachment." The V.A.D. was a group of wartime volunteer medical workers.
2. A.R.P. stands for "Air Raid Precautions." The A.R.P. was a government organization dedicated to protecting civilians from the dangers of air raids.

TWO

CHRIST AN UNREALITY

Could even God have done more than he has done to prove that he is real?—to prove that he has a sensitive human heart and wants to be treated as one who is human!

Did he not become a baby needing a woman's devoted care? Did he not shed tears openly over the personal sorrow of his friends' death? Did he not reveal frankly that a small discourtesy had hurt him in the Pharisee's house and express pathetic gratitude to a sinful woman who came there to comfort him? Did he not reproach his apostles, sleeping during his agony? With his dying breath did he not speak of his thirst, of the anguish of his soul?

Yet we often treat him as if he did not exist, as if he were not real at all!

I speak to the virtuosa of the spiritual life, to the expert in spirituality with her network of rules and mortifications, her notebooks and hieroglyphics and all the rest. Don't be an expert in spiritual life. Treat Christ as the real Person that he is, don't fuss and worry about your soul.

Would it please you if one of whom you were passionately fond, with whom you lived, to whom you devoted yourself completely, was so busy dusting the ornaments in the house that she never had a moment to listen to you, or indeed to notice that you were there!

We all know the woman who is exaggeratedly house-proud, who concentrates on the neatness, cleanliness, beauty of her house, to the exclusion of its comfort. Her house is not a home, nothing must ever be left about, out of place. To come in with muddy shoes is a crime, it is a crime to disarrange the cushions! In such a house one can neither work nor rest, one is never at home, because it is not a home.

There are many women who are "soul-proud" in the same way. They spend their whole time cleaning up their soul, turning out the rubbish, dusting and polishing. Like the house-proud woman they become nervous, tired, there is nothing left in them to give, they have wasted themselves on the silver, the curtains, the ornaments.

Christ wants to be at home in your soul. He will not go away and leave you if the house is chilly and uncomfortable; he loves you too much to leave you, but how often, how tragically often, he must say nowadays: "The Son of Man has nowhere to lay his head."

Christ asks for a home in your soul, where he can be at rest with you, where he can talk easily to you, where you and he, alone together, can laugh and be silent and be delighted with one another.

All this may seem daring, but it is true, it is the meaning of the Incarnation; we should all realise that it is true were it not that for years and years Christ has been treated as if he were not real at all.

Now it is impossible to imagine anyone in any human relationship enduring, let alone being pleased by, the things we do to please God!

This can only be realised by imagining the very same things in a profound human relationship. Picture to yourself a husband and wife. The husband, out at work, has thought all day long of his wife, he has been longing to go home, to tell her of his love, to spend a long delightful evening with her. He has brought a little gift for her to prove to her—if proof be needed—that wherever he is, his thoughts fly to her. He starts eagerly for home, expecting that she will come to greet him, will light up with joy at his first words and will be ready to sit down and rest, while in his own way he tells her all he has been thinking and doing all day.

He listens for her step coming to the door. She does not come. He calls her. There is no answer. What is wrong? He goes in to find her sitting dejectedly in the corner scribbling, she does not look up at first, then with averted eyes and hanging head she advances and offers him a sheet of paper. He looks, reads, the greeting dies on his lips, in dismay he sees this—

"List of the little things I have done to-day which may offend you:

I spilt a drop of milk (value about half a cent).

I folded your shirts a little carelessly.

I allowed my mind to wander from the thought of you twice while preparing your dinner.

I allowed a shirt button to remain under the chest of drawers and bought another in place of it," and so on—

"My dear," says the poor man, "are you feeling ill?"

"Wait!" she says, a gleam of melancholy joy in her eyes, "I have another list." She produces another paper and he reads:

"Pin-pricks provoked for you to-day:

Pricked my finger on purpose while darning your socks.

Refrained from turning on the wireless.

Ate nauseating cheap lunch.

Allowed the baby to cry all day without stopping."

A bleak chill wraps the husband's soul; he sits down silently: "What is wrong," he thinks, "have I proved such a brute that she actually thinks all this can please me?— and my poor little child left crying too?—perhaps she is ill." He is going to question her tactfully when suddenly and more brightly she hands him another list.

"All the things I want you to give me."

It is a long list; while he reads it she turns on the wireless, and the evening passes. The lovely evening is lost. He knows only one thing—he does not understand—they are miles and miles apart—they are both alone.

Christ understands, he can even smile at these efforts to please him, but the fact remains, if you treat him like that, then in your soul "the Son of Man has nowhere to lay his head."

"Behold," he says, "I stand at the door and knock."

If we love without response, if we may not express our love, it is unendurable—we have to go away, to forget. Christ never goes away, never forgets, all day long, wherever you are, whoever you are, whatever you are doing, his whole heart is concentrated upon you.

He watches you with the eye of a mother watching an only child. He sees not the surface things, not the imperfections inevitable to human frailty, but the truly lovable in you, your dependence on him, your need of him. Does a mother love her child less when its hair is tousled, does she love her child less because it has fallen and bruised itself? No, indeed; only, if that is possible, more!

What then must we do?

Listen. Be silent. Let Christ speak to you. Forget yourself, forget your soul, let him tell you how he loves you, show you what he is like, prove to you that he is real. Silence in your soul means a gentle attention to Christ, it means turning away from self to him, it means looking at him, listening to him.

God speaks silently, he speaks in your heart; if your heart is noisy, chattering, you will not hear.

Every ordinary thing in your life is a word of his love, your home, your work, the clothes you wear, the air you breathe, the food you eat, the friends you delight in, the flowers under your feet are the courtesy of his heart flung down to you! All these things say one thing only:

"See how I love you."

He asks only one thing, that you will let him tell you this, directly, simply; that you will treat him as someone real, not as someone who does not really exist.

CHRIST A REALITY

IN ETERNITY

Christ always existed. He did not begin to exist in 1 A.D. and cease to exist in 33 A.D.

He is the Second Person of the Blessed Trinity. He is one with the Father and the Paraclete.

Between the three Persons of the Blessed Trinity there is illimitable love. Hate and fear began in time and will end in time. Love always has been and always will be, because God is love.

The creation of the world is the inevitable result of the love between the three Persons of the Blessed Trinity. Man is made in the image of that love. Christ is the Word of God; he is the Word of God speaking his love, uttering him, telling his love to the world.

The truth of a spoken word does not die in the person who uttered it. The word has gone from him, its truth has entered another mind, it is now alive in someone else, but it remains in the being of the speaker. Christ is God's Word, saying to the world: "I love you." That creative truth has entered the world and become the life, of the world, but Christ also remains in God and is not separated from him.

Christ is the Word of God, his life on earth is the lyric, the love-song of God, first uttered on earth through Mary of Nazareth. Infinite music in a little reed.

OUR LADY

His coming was foretold on David's strings of gold, cried aloud on the tongues of prophets cleansed by fire, but when he came the Word of God was less than a whispered word, muted to the sound of tears and tuned to human ears. It was simply the beating of a virgin's heart.

Christ asked Mary of Nazareth for her human nature. For her littleness, her limitations, flesh and blood and bone, five senses, hands and feet, a human heart.

He, who was invulnerable, asked to be able to feel cold and heat, hunger and thirst, weariness and pain. He who had all things and had made all things, asked to be able to be poor and to labour with his hands and look with wonder at the wild flowers. He who was wholly sufficient to himself asked Mary to give him a heart that might be broken.

Mary answered "yes." To make his body she gave her body, for his humanity, her humanity. The first utterance in this world of the Word of God was less than the infant's wail that it waxed to, it was the heart of Christ beating in a girl's heart.

Our Lady answered "yes" to Christ; she answered for us all; she was quite human. Had he asked her for anything else but her littleness she could not have given it, because she had nothing else.

She gave him human nature, our human nature; the Incarnation means that Christ gave himself to human nature to be its supernatural life, as the seed gives its life to the dark hard earth. Christ, sown in the soil of Mary's humanity, was the seed given to human nature, to flower in countless lives, to be unnumbered springs, flowering, harvest, resurrections of the human heart.

Love has no limits. Christ desired not only to suffer and rejoice in one man but in all men.

Our Lady has only one Child, but she is the mother of all men, she is the Mother of Christ.

Mary was an empty reed to receive the love song of the Word of God, only the breath of God uttered the song through her, it is the song of all the laughter and all the tears in the world, the Shepherd's song piping to his sheep.

THE INCARNATION

Christ was not an apparition, a spirit clothed as a man. He was a man. His life on earth was made up of ordinary things, made extraordinary by love. He used the common substance, flesh and blood, body and soul. He worked and ate and slept. He earned his living, with the joys, exultations, fatigues of other men. Had you gone to visit him at his home in Nazareth you would have found him like other men, but giving a significance to ordinary things that others often fail to do.

Imagine such a visit, imagine it without the sentimentality that often treacles over this sort of thinking. It is evening, you have come to supper. He is putting away his tools, unconsciously he smiles at the burnish on them; you see how he loves his tools. On the floor by the bench there are wood shavings, how clean and fine they are, curled like yellow petals, those are the shavings that only the sharpest plane cuts—what a craftsman he is! What a beautiful thing work is, seen from this Man's angle! He sits down in the doorway, you with him, you notice the signs of the day's fatigue, good fatigue that seeps out of one in the evening. He wipes the sweat from his face, his eyes are a little tired, they have the intensity of eyes that use the last ray of light. Yes, he works hard, he gives good measure!

He is looking now at the flowers. You follow his glance, you notice things you had never seen before, how pale and shadowless white flowers are in the dusk! A smell of

cooking fills the room, a good savoury smell, it is comforting; he will enjoy the meal he has earned. Work and
joy are things that make one hungry! Yes, after all, there is
poetry in work, he has enjoyed the day, has rejoiced in the
skill of his hands, in the stretch and ripple of his muscles,
in the unique smell of the walnut wood, in the touch of
the smooth polished surface of the thing made, when he
has done. What splendour, what majesty of soul and body
there is after all in work! In this Man's company what a
lovely thing life is!

He looks at you silently, smiling, a great stillness is on
you. Gradually you understand. The human life of his is
yours. He has put on your life as we put on an old worn
garment, liking it better for its shabbiness, for the ease
with which we can work in it and sit comfortably in it, a
garment like a friend that can rough it with us; yes, so he
has put on our life, your life, like an old garment and he
has worn it to his shape, moulded it by his body, by his
actions, to a thing of unspeakable beauty.

All day long, and every day of his life, he has been
moulding your humanity to his pattern, his shape. All day
he has been doing more, even more than that, he has been
moulding himself to your shape, giving himself to you,
living your life. Every moment has been a self-donation
to you; the joy and anxiety of his work, the strength and
the effort of his body, the sight of his eyes, the touch of his
hands, the concentration of his thought. While eating he
replenished his life for you; while resting he rested his life

for you; asleep in the darkness, his sleep was one long act
of love, renewing his life for you.

CHRIST IS STILL HERE

After his resurrection Christ did not leave us. He is still
on earth, in the blessed sacrament and in us. Our life is
sacramental, we are Christ's final sacrament.

Christ used the flesh and blood of Mary for his life
on earth, the Word of love was uttered in her heart-beat.
Christ used his own body to utter his love on earth, his
perfectly real body, with bone and sinew and blood and
tears; Christ uses our bodies to express his love on earth,
our humanity. For all practical purposes in this, life soul
and body are one, through the common dust of our
humanity Christ remains here to express his love.

A Christian life is a sacramental life, it is not a life lived
only in the mind, only by the soul; through the bodies of
men and women Christ toils and endures and rejoices and
loves and dies; in them he is increased, set free, impris-
oned, restrained, in them he is crucified and buried and
rises from the dead.

Our humanity is the substance of the sacramental life
of Christ in us, like the wheat for the Host, like the grape
for the Chalice.

Christ works his love through material as well as spiritual things. Into his worship, following his own lead, the
Church, his Church, brings material things, pure wax,

flame, oil, salt, gold, water, linen, the voices of men, the gestures and actions of men, our own souls and bodies—the substance of our flesh and blood. All this is consistent with the Incarnation, when Christ took the human nature of Our Lady to be himself.

WHAT THE CHURCH IS

The Church is everyone who is part of Christ on earth, everyone who is included in Christ's sacramental life in us.

Christ makes us part of his sacramental life by giving his life to be the life of our souls. He is in each one of his own completely because he cannot be incomplete. He is in each separate Host whole, not divided, and so in each man in whom he is the life. Therefore, since he cannot be separated from himself or severed or parted from himself, we are all one.

We are one body, Christ. His life in us is like the bloodstream in the body, a torrent which flows through the whole body into each part continually. To each part it gives life in the right proportion; where there is need it repairs and heals, using even waste matter in the process. This image of the bloodstream as the life of Christ is very apt, for the blood gives life, colour, beauty to each part, and the same which tingles in the extremities continually passes through the heart. So is Christ's life in man, a torrent reaching to those who seem far off, to all kinds of men, a life-stream, always vigorous and pure at heart which drives it through the whole body.

The same life in popes, saints, the souls in purgatory, kings, clerks, wise men, fools, labourers, sinners, old people and children, in everyone, making them one.

What one Christian does affects every other, as one part of the body affects the whole body. No Christian can act alone, as he is part of a whole. This oneness was compared to the body by St. Paul.

Christ himself compared it to a vine: "I am the vine, you the branches."

The oneness of all Christians in Christ is not at all like the kind of oneness in human groups or organizations. It is not imposed from above, it is not artificial, it does not produce a "type" of human being, it has no standard pattern. It is organic, it has the quality of growing and flowering. It is indeed like the vine, including in one life infinite diversity of lives.

The vine thrusts great roots down into the earth, taking hold of it in the darkness; the sap rises in the rough, hard trunk, flows out into the bright, fresh leaves and clusters of fruit, and on and on to the slenderest branch, to the tenderest bud, to the tendril farthest away from the root, the most delicate wisp of life. But that frailest extremity is as strong as the trunk, as alive, for its life is the same sap; just as the tip of the little finger lives by the life of the heart's blood.

The Church is Christ in men, men in Christ, on earth, in purgatory, in heaven. On earth it is the Christ-life manifest in the crudest and most sensitive, the simplest and most sophisticated, the strongest and the weakest, the saint and the sinner: expressed through man's humanity, his body and soul, his hands and mind and heart, his plough and his sword, his books and his music, his tears and his laughter, in his surrenders, in his renunciations, the tenderest whispering of his loves, in his births and his deaths.

"I am the vine—you the branches." The Church is the Christ-life, the root of man's being, the fruit of his life, the opening of his frailest bud.

THE POETRY OF CHRIST

The modern world has opposed poetry. A mechanized world, a world of greed, a world at war, hard youth, art itself soulless and hard, all this is against poetry, the wonder of life.

Christ keeps poetry alive in the world, in its essence and in its outward form. The Liturgy of the Church is the form in which Christ, God's word of love, is sung continuously.

There is the rhythm of Christ, the Christ-voice, the continual utterance of the Word on earth.

Rhythm is not mere repetition. It is the gathering of energy to the culmination of its own intensity. It moves in a cycle, spending its life only in renewing it.

The rhythm of Christ is love moving on a circle of light from birth to death from death to resurrection.

In creation it is shadowed. The seasons move from spring—life young and new—summer and flowering, autumn seeding and sowing, and winter covering the sown seed with the white snows while it grows to another spring.

It is in each day of our life just the same rhythm: waking, working, falling asleep, sleeping to wake again.

Christ's life on earth is the complete circle of that rhythm; the rhythm continues in our life.

Life is ruled by a musical law. A procession of life moves through the world; children, here yesterday, are gone; the men and women they have become are passing. The old people they will be vanish like autumn leaves on the wind's drift, and the wind's drift will seed the world.

For as long as it lasts the world will be thronged with children, mature people and old people; for those who live, pass, life remains. Christ goes on, the stream of life, War can kill living people, it can destroy civilizations, it cannot end life, man can destroy his own works, he cannot touch God's.

The rhythm of the liturgical year is a natural expression of man's life in Christ. It is like the days and the nights, like waking and sleeping, like the procession from childhood to resurrection.

At Christmas, Christ is born in us. At Passiontide, he suffers and dies in us. At Pentecost, the name of the love of his spirit is kindled in us. Advent returns, Christ with it, to his secret life in us, to be born into the world again.

THE CHRIST VOICE

Christ is born in us, works in us, loves in us, dies in us. In him we are one.

He is our strength and our poetry. God has given us a Christ-voice. The Word of God, saying "I love you" to men is now heard in heaven saying "I love you" to God. It is the Christ-voice, saying what is dumb in man's heart. The words used in the ceaseless prayer of the Church are man's age-long poetry, theirs is unearthly splendour which mixes with the hymning of the seraphim. But the themes are those of the earth's primitive folksongs: birth, love, death and resurrection.

The song of the cradle and the cross. The feast of spring, the feast of harvest.

The voice is not only that of the contemplative chanting the Office, the priest saying Mass. It is not only the voice of those whose lives are given to tuning their hearts to utter Christ's prayer. No, it is the voice of the dumb, the inarticulate, all over the world. It is the voice of the worker; of the busy man, passing in the street; of the clerk bending over his books in the office.

It is for the man in the world that the contemplative utters Christ's prayers day and night.

It is for the contemplative in his solitude that the worker toils and talks in the crowd, day and night. It is not only the priest who consecrates the Host day after day, it is also every man and woman and child who gives his body, his humanity, his substance for the miracle to God. And always for all, for priest and layman, for sinner and saint, for the eloquent and the inarticulate, the Christ-voice speaks to God.

The Church gives us this Christ-voice. Look for a moment at a London church, late on a winter's afternoon. There is a young mother, helping her child to pray. The child forgets; she holds his hands folded in her own, the child glances at the Tabernacle, he would like to say good night to God, but his thoughts are away like a flock of birds in the twilight, and his head, heavy with sleep, lolls on his mother's shoulder. She smiles, and says good night for him.

Away in his stall a monk lifts a clear voice from the heart of eternal childhood; his is the Christ-voice saying good night to the Father of Christ.

We are all children, our words difficult, our thoughts scattered, but the Church folds our hands in hers and utters our prayer.

Christ is in us all; his life, his labour, his poetry, his prayer. He is not divided. The man in the world with his burden of care, the man in the cloister with his peace and his crown of thorns, all are one Christ. The man who works, toils with the hands of the man who prays; the man who prays folds the worker's hands in his.

So it is that Christ is in us, acting and yet resting, his hands lifted and yet toiling, nailed to the cross and yet healing. His feet are nailed to the cross above life's flowering meadows, and yet they are walking the common streets of all the cities in the world, the Shepherd's feet following his wandering sheep.

The heart of Christ is always alone in the white solitude of peace, yet always assailed and breaking over new Jerusalems.

So it is that Christ is a reality, the Reality of the Infinite God, and the reality of our own lives, our own joy and sorrow and work and sacrifice and love.

"I, if I be lifted up, will draw all things to me."

THREE

THE COMFORTING OF CHRIST

We are all "other Christs"—but not all know it, and in this great passion of his going on now, we shall act in different parts as all those who entered into his first passion did.

For some, comfort lies in knowing that they are one with him and can face everything, knowing that he, Who is in them, has overcome the world; "Fear not, for I have overcome the world." But others get comfort in knowing their "otherness," that they are also other than him. The expression is clumsy, for literally we are "in" him, but we have an "otherness" too, and this makes us able to approach him and to comfort him objectively. Whatever we do now, we did to Christ in his passion; that is hard to grasp, but true. All things are always present to him, time is not as we think it is, and to-day was present to him two thousand years ago.

In Gethsemane he saw our world now, and feared with our fear, and the angel who brought him the chalice brought all that any of us would do to comfort him. We do truly comfort him most when, recognizing him in our neighbour, we serve and love our neighbour for the love of him. All that we do in the war ought to be done with that single idea, it is real war work and real worship. Put his love into everything. It is not only saints who comfort Christ, sinners can do it, all sorts of people; in his passion all are drawn together in one act of suffering and love.

This comes home when we think of those who comforted him in his historical passion, and of their counterpart, who are comforting him in his mystical body now. They are not one type, not all good, they are just all who know how to love: a middle-class married woman, a woman of Jerusalem, a notorious prostitute, a dying thief, a pure boy, a soldier, a rich councillor—a motley lot of people! They make us realize that there are none, rich or poor, respectable or not, sound or ill, who cannot take part in the passion and comfort Christ; and they comfort by receiving as well as by giving, passively as well as actively. It is by loving and being loved that we can endure to-day.

Simon of Cyrene, who took up the cross unwillingly, "they made him." There are Simons now, unwilling conscripts forced to enter the war, to face its awful reality; conscripts of all kinds, even "war workers" forced by public opinion. If they realize that this is all just helping Christ to carry his cross, by taking their full share in the heavy burden that has fallen on humanity, then they become truly Simons, and will share the glory of helping Christ.

Veronica, who wiped the blood and dirt from his face. Many literally have her great privilege, all who have the courage to help the wounded, clean their wounds, nurse them, all those who are wiping the tears and sweat and blood from the face of Christ.

The good thief, who turned to him with utter trust and humility, and seeing his Goodness, knew Who he was and asked him for mercy. There are thousands who have lost their faith, gone wrong, drifted from him, who are sinners, or have been. Now being crucified, instead of cursing at this bitter fate, they, seeing that it is the innocents who bear the most, will confess humbly that for themselves to suffer would be just, and turn to Christ even at the last. These comfort him exceedingly, it was for them he came, for them he died. They save their souls by recognizing him in the innocents.

The centurion, who witnessed his death, and cried out, "Indeed this man was the Son of God!" All who witness Christ in the fortitude and endurance of his members and know him in the brave dying or suffering of a fellow-worker or a brother-in-arms, and are converted—these comfort him and prove his sacrifice in his members is not in vain. These are his glory.

John, the beloved boy, who followed Christ to the cross and became the foster son of his mother. Everyone who for the love of Christ is kind to the widows and mothers of this war, and who gives them shelter or material help, sympathy or comfort, all of them are beloved by him, like John. They comfort him extremely by being trustees of those whom he loves.

His mother. Every mother now is the mother of Christ, and of those we can speak only with the reverence with which we speak of Our Lady, she suffered his passion with him, all of it. All the mothers who have given their sons as "other Christs" to redeem the world, and who, because they are mothers, must suffer all that their children suffer, these are comforting Christ as his own mother did; she who was, and is, his supreme comforter.

Mary Magdalene, who was a sinner but braved the scorn of everyone and readily followed him to his death. She consoled him with her love, the sheer lovely extravagance of it, her genius for doing what was moving and tender, and her courage in love. All who, though they are full of sin, nevertheless pour out real love on others and make other people's lives sweeter by showing them that they are loved, by gifts of the heart as precious as the spikenard, though to the world's eyes as useless.

Joseph of Arimathea. Many of us may have to give Christ in man the reverence due to the dead Christ, all of us must make our hearts tombs where he may rest, and we must have such still, peaceful hearts that all who are exhausted and near defeat will find stillness and rest and fortitude in us, and peace bringing them to resurrection. So shall we be like Joseph; rich indeed in giving Christ a place to rest. All those people were present to Christ when the angel came to him in his agony and made him strong, made him able to face the passion. Their love was the chalice from which Christ drank. They did only what he commanded when he said: "Little children, love one another."

The Angel of the Agony. I ought to have put the angel first, but I have left him till last because all of us together, all trying to drink from our Lord's chalice, all trying to comfort him in his passion in his members, all of us together can be this great angel who was sent by God to comfort Christ. In Gethsemane, Christ let us see a glimpse of him just as he would be in man, suffering in his mystical body, wholly human, afraid, sweating with fear, weak physically, shocked, down on the ground, praying to be let off. Just as we are when the passion faces us; but the angel came and comforted him, made him strong. What did this angel bring, what was the chalice from which Christ drank and grew strong?

Surely it was the love, the little efforts to comfort him, that we should offer to-day, the accumulated tears of Magdalene, the wonder of the centurion, the strong arms of Simon, the mothering of the world's mothers, the treasure of the quiet peace of the Josephs of Arimathea. It was just our love, making us able to use that sort of kindness and skill and charity to each other, which can now give strength to Christ on earth and crown him king in us.

THE WORDS ON THE CROSS

It is never easy to meditate on the passion; the more we know of real sorrow and real pain, the more we see of suffering, the more difficult it becomes to think about the pain and sorrow of Christ.

Indeed, it becomes impossible, because once we know inwardly, with our hearts, not only with our minds, how real Christ is—and what suffering is—we can no longer bear to have beautiful thoughts about the suffering Christ. The mind becomes bleak, we begin to suffer with him—and that is what real meditation on the passion always becomes, suffering with him.

It is more than that, it is actually Christ suffering in us. We are united to him, we are one, and it is when his passion becomes real to us, through experience and love, that we grow aware of his presence in us. But for this presence of Christ, his living in us, his actually being our life, we could not bear the things which have actually happened to some, indeed to many, and which are more than a threat to everyone. We can bear them for one reason only, because Christ, Who is identified with us, Who is in us, has already suffered and overcome everything that we shall suffer, or ever can suffer.

We cannot shed a tear, but that tear has already blinded the eyes of Christ. We cannot be without tears, but that constriction of the heart has constricted his Heart. He has known all and every kind of fear that we know, and there is no possible loneliness, no agony of separation, but it is Christ's; indeed, not one of us can die, but it is Christ dying. And Christ, Who faces all these things in our lives, has overcome them all and has sanctified them by his limitless love. His love made every moment of his passion redeeming and healing and life-giving, and this love, this Christ-love, is ours, just as much as his suffering is.

We are now beginning in very earnest to experience the contemplation which consists in suffering with Christ, and the way to sanctify it is not so much to suffer with him as to ask him to let us realize that he it is Who suffers in us. For, this understood, we cannot help abandoning our will to his completely, and letting him suffer in us in *his way,* and his way is the way of love. Complete though it is, in his grief there is no bitterness; and what seems to be frustration and waste is not, it is fruitful; this is because every moment of his passion is informed by love.

Our work is to love too, to love always, to love everyone, and to love to the end.

The words spoken by Our Lord on the cross reveal far more than we can hope to grasp; they are in themselves enough to show us how to live through his experience of his passion which is the war. That is the only excuse for tearing the mind away from its direct, unthinking acceptance of our present suffering, to consider some of Christ's words on the cross, one by one.

"FATHER, FORGIVE THEM, FOR THEY KNOW NOT WHAT THEY DO"

This is how we must love our enemy: ask God to forgive them. There is no question of our forgiving--that must be understood. We are sinners, like them, like them we have crucified Christ. Christ himself never said that he forgave, never asked for an apology. His delicacy was so great, he made it easy for people who were ashamed. "The bruised reed I will not crush." His forgiveness could be taken for granted. His love included it, always, obviously. His wonderful delicacy always proved it. To Peter: "Lovest thou Me?" not, "Do you apologize?" To the apostles who had fled in his dire need of them, "Peace be to you." Every reunion tactful, loving, saving the other one's feelings.

"Father, forgive them." His own forgiveness proved by this, that he is dying for them. And what had to be forgiven? The injustice, the brutality, the treachery. The sin to God, Whom he adored, the blasphemy, the sacrilege, the shame, the great crowd against one and that One innocent. The cowardice. Not only what they did to him, it was harder to forgive what they did to his mother and to his friends. It is harder to forgive for others than for oneself.

He wanted to suffer for them, not for them to suffer for him. "Whom seek ye? I am he—let these go their way!" But the dearest of all were made to suffer it all, the dearest friends, John and Magdalene, and above all Mary, his mother. She had to see it all, to hear the crowd, the blasphemies, the insults, see the wounds, the nakedness, suffer it all in herself because she loved him: her very love made to be a sorrow to them both. Yet he forgave, he asked forgiveness for what they did to those he loved.

We are angry, we do not know how to endure the cruelty of the enemy to innocent people. "If the hatred is for us, fight us, it is we whom you seek, let these others alone." It is hard to forgive what is done to others, even when we don't know them—and when we do?

But Christ had all this, and infinitely more, to forgive. He did it for love of us. We will do it for love of him, and we will do it with the power of his love in us. "Without Me, you can do nothing." But with You, Lord, we can forgive everything!

The excuse he made, "they know not what they do"— that was true then, and it is true now in precisely the same way. Of course they knew that they were tormenting and killing a man, but they did not know Who the Man was, that it was God.

They do not know now, they do not know that every blow is aimed at Christ, that whatever is done to anyone is done to him. "How long have I been with you, and you have not known me?" It is not only for our enemy he prayed, but for us too, and we do not know him, in everyone. We miss him, pass him by; he lives in everyone, and we run a great danger of forgetting, and excluding many from our love, not recognizing him. But at least, in the power of his love, from the will, from the heart, every day we can repeat his words: "Father, forgive them, for they know not what they do."

"Woman, Behold Thy Son"

This love passes everything. Who should comfort his mother but himself? Who should take her arm, lead her away from all this, hold her hand, take her home? Surely he should.

His hands are nailed. He is helpless—helpless to help her. That is the measure of his love for us. The anguish we all know, our helplessness to help others, even to reach them, in some sorrows. She was out of his reach.

"He has saved others, himself He cannot save." Worse, far worse, to one who has loved as he loved, he cannot save Mary or comfort her; how it would comfort her if she could ease his sorrow! If he could lay that thorn-crowned head on her breast, if he could come to her and let her dress those wounds! And how it would comfort him to comfort her!

It is hard to say "No";—absurd to call it hard—words fail.

It is even harder to give the joy to another, to make someone else her son. John can take her hand, make her a home, buy her clothes and food, amuse her, comfort her, gradually make it easy to sit with her in the evenings and talk about him, her Son, who was killed. Another son— that is the hard thing!

But the love of this Son is perfect love, unselfish. We can't understand unselfish love. We have never known it. "Son, behold your mother!" But, in his strength, we shall have to do it, have to commit our dearest to others, to keep our hands nailed to the cross of our duty, to keep our feet nailed in the way God has chosen, forgoing over and over again the longing to be elsewhere and essential to someone we love, to be depended on by that one person.

His love, perfect, unselfish, thirsting and natural though it is, makes the dearest independent, gives them happiness when happiness seems impossible, through pure unselfishness. Only his life in us can purify our hearts and make such love, or something faintly like it, possible to us. Purify our hearts, Christ, perfect love! Make our sacrifice a sacrificing love.

"My God, My God, Why Hast Thou Forsaken Me?"

Is there any other occasion on which he calls his Father, God:—addresses him as his God?

This is an act of faith, something we don't understand and can't probe. But we can learn something, that he did experience the feeling of despair, that he did reach the rock-bottom of misery, humiliation, fear and sorrow, that he really did suffer all that we can. He was as human as we, his love had to empty him out to the last dreg of life—and in that moment he professes aloud and confesses to the Godhead of his Father. "My God."

When we despair, when we say, "there is no God," we do not say how far we have gone from him, what outcasts we have become. Christ's love is otherwise, in his misery he must proclaim the Being of God, his own faith in God: such is his love for God. And he must despair—that is the limit of mental grief—that measures his love for me.

Christ, grant us, when all seems lost, when there seems no hope any more, to acknowledge our God, Who is our hope, Who is All that is. In Your Name we believe in God: "Though he should slay me, yet will I trust in him."

"IT IS CONSUMMATED"

This is the expression of the joy of love. This does not mean: "I am finished" "I am exhausted." It means, the sacrifice is perfect, the work is completed, the passion is perfected, the seed has been sown, I have come to the fullness of my being, and now I, who am love, in this perfection of all you willed me to be, am at last consumed in my love. "I have finished the work that you gave me to do."

What was it? How like ours it was, this work, this life of Christ on earth! Some happy years, childhood and the voice and touch and smell of the mother, her warmth and laughter and gentleness. Some years of work in obscurity. Then the fasting and the public life, the life without rest, always the crowd, always the critics, always someone to find fault. And the healing, the blind to be given light, the lepers to be made clean, the poor to be comforted—and all of it ending in what? The cross; the work a failure; all the gentleness, all the poetry and beauty of it ending in this—violence, brutality, death.

"It is consummated." That is not failure. That is success. The gentleness, the humility, the courage, the generosity, all are consummated, perfect, complete, and all are offered and accepted in sacrifice. "I have overcome the world." "Fear not, little flock, it has pleased your heavenly Father to give you a kingdom."

We, strange as it is, live lives analogous to his. We, too, must be consummated. His love in us, given to us to save the world, this must come, too, to its fullness, and love will overcome all things through the forgiveness, the longing, the courtesy, the bigness, the faith and the wholeness, of Our Lord, Jesus Christ.

Give us this grace, Lord, to consummate Your love in every single thought and act, to bring the fullness of Your love to be the consummation of everything we do.

"Father, into Thy Hands I Commend My Spirit"

It begins and ends with "Father." "Father, forgive them." He is our Father, Father of all of us, of Britons, Poles, Finns, Germans, Russians, Dutch, French Belgians, everyone; and he loves us all with a Father's love, all of us. We all grieve our Father, we all need his forgiveness.

"Father, into Thy Hands I commend my spirit." I think I once heard a scholar say that in the original Hebrew it reads: "Father, in Thy hands I bury my head." Perfect trust, he is going to die; this is complete surrender, this is the adoring Son, literally putting himself into his Father's hands.

"Under us are the Eternal Arms." Ours, too, is the spirit of Christ, literally; and now in a world as dark, as confusing, as strange as the hour of death, how shall we keep the integrity, the sweetness, the tenderness of the Spirit of Christ, our trust?

We are with him on the cross, helpless, helpless to help, helpless in every way, bound to go through with our passion, bound to face it with his love. We have nothing else, no wisdom, no courage of our own, nothing. But we have his love. Who, however, shall keep it for us, what breath keep its flame bright, burning in this cruel storm, what wind give it shade? Who is there gentle enough to keep its delicacy for us, who strong enough to defend its valour, who noble enough to keep its chivalry? Our trust, the Spirit of Christ, in a world that assails it.

Our heavenly Father alone can keep it, in his hands it is safe, strong to forgive, to heal, to purify, to love. The power of the love of Our Lord. "Father, into Thy hands I commend my Spirit."

THE STATIONS OF THE CROSS

There are many angles from which an artist can design the Stations of the Cross. If he attempts an historical representation, his work is doomed to fail in its purpose. The Church, for reasons of reverence, founded on sad experience, forbids a too realistic representation of Christ in his passion.

Far from limiting the artist in his work, this deepens the scope of it. It compels him to choose aspects of the passion which are not limited by time but continue in the world; to see the passion as something taking place now.

He will not belittle the part bodily pain has taken in our redemption, but he will see the same redeeming element in our pain, so much less than Christ's but included in his. He will realize the passion in the mind of Christ and how that continues in us, from the pope shepherding a broken world to a child weeping over a broken doll.

His work will serve its purpose only if he comes to it from meditation and prayer, from sympathetic experience of men, women and children, in great humility and restraint. His problem is how to say as little as he can without saying nothing at all.

The Church is a mother teaching her children from a picture book. Before there were printed books, and before laymen could read, they learned the faith from the pictures that covered the walls of our churches.

Now the Stations of the Cross are almost all that is left of that tradition. Providence has so arranged it, because

learning from pictures means thinking out the meaning
for ourselves, discovering with our hearts, and there is no
way of learning the passion of Christ except through the
adventure of our own heart.

When we were children, we had in our nursery a picture of a fairy castle with a little road winding round it,
vanishing in mists behind some hills. We used to spend
hours and hours imagining where this road led to—in our
imagination we walked into the picture and discovered
the secret valley behind the hills. Each one of us made a
different discovery, one found a town, another a village,
another an enchanted wood. We all had different adventures on the way, we met our own giants and dragons, discovered our own enchantments and were helped by our
own magicians and fairies.

We should be able to approach the Stations of the
Cross in the same way, but with one difference. Our valley
was a dream valley, our adventures on the way part of the
endless "let's pretend" of childhood. The Stations of the
Cross are real, their road is the road to Calvary, the adventures on the way to it are the truest experience of which
we are capable, and it leads to the one reality, Christ.

However little the artist puts down for us to look at,
however simple his finished picture, it must show an
essential truth. A friend of mine attempted a historically
accurate set, but after long research decided that he could
be certain only of the pattern of Pilate's sandal. He painted Pilate's sandal with such skill and detail that one simply could not look at anything else.

That is not what I mean by essential truth. A picture of, say, the twelfth station, could show just Our Lord on the cross alone, leaving out the two thieves, the crowds, those at the foot of the cross. That would not be an accurate historical picture, but it would symbolize a truth, the utter loneliness of Christ on the cross. Or it might suggest other thoughts—questions such as: "Why was Christ on the cross?" "Unless the seed fall to the earth . . ." and so on. Unlimited possibilities—but all would start from the one brief point of an essential truth.

There are people who do not find it necessary to use words or ideas for meditation. We know that we can hear a song, sung in a language of which we know not one word, but if the rhythm, the melody of it finds an answer in our heart, it echoes from our own soul. We can understand it without being able to translate a word of it into our own speech.

For some, prayer is like that. The muted music of the human, suffering Christ touches a responsive chord in their own being. They do not require words and images, and indeed cannot use them. They cannot explain. They have no words, even for Christ. Perhaps they do not understand the music themselves. Perhaps if they uttered it aloud it would only confuse the world. It would not sound in their voice as it sounds in their souls. Occasionally the childhood of love taught by Christ gives to other souls than those a like simplicity, a direct approach. Once, when I had given a set of Stations of my own to a convent, I asked a very old lay-sister, on whose verdict I hung my hopes, what she thought of them. "Well, dear," she said, "they do not worry me as they do some of the other nuns, because I always shut my eyes to say my prayers."

But there are others who do like to look at the pictures and who look at them many times before they, too, learn to shut their eyes to say their prayers.

I am going to look at a few pictures now and write down just what comes into my head, single words, short phrases, whatever they suggest to me; this I shall do, hoping that others, distracted like myself, may discover their own starting point from such elementary meditations.

May that starting-point close their eyes one day on everything but Christ, Whom they will see then, not with the eyes only, not only on a crude picture, but everywhere, in everyone, in everything, and not least in their own darkness.

Christ is condemned, more by weakness than by malice. Pilate is more weak than sinful, yet, uneasy, aware of the injustice. "I see no cause in this just man."

The real reason? Pilate's position, his prestige, his income. "Are you Caesar's friend?" He has nothing against Christ, even contempt for his enemies. But—Caesar's friend, I wash my hands of it!

Can I condemn Pilate? If it meant my job, my social position, my income, should I not perhaps compromise? Never, it is true, in malice, but how often in weakness! "Let him be crucified." If it means even the moral courage to go to Mass from a week-end party, or to keep the fasting and abstinence? If it means a little denial to pay my bills promptly, or to be just in my dealings? Do I never wash my hands of him to humour the majority, to placate those to whom I am abject, even though in my heart of hearts I despise them?

More weak than sinful, more in cowardice than in malice, yet—uneasy, aware of the injustice, how often do I crucify Christ in my soul, condemn him to death?

Christ receives his cross, not only the heavy wood two thousand years ago, but the suffering of all times. The conditions of to-day, of the whole world's pain, of the poverty and sweating and grief in my city, and my personal grief. The cross was there before. He did not give us the cross, but he gave us himself on the cross. Receiving his cross, he changed it from heavy lifeless wood to the flowering tree that should bear fruit in all generations.

Receiving his cross, we receive him.

Jesus Falls under the Cross

Jesus, who? God himself. The invulnerable! He has deliberately made himself man that he may be hurt, may be wounded, may be weak. Why?—for sinners, for the weak, for the hurt. He wants to be like them, to show it.

"I came not to save the just, but sinners."

Jesus *falls.* He could have been an example to the strong; an example of "mind over matter," of stoicism, he could have gone on miraculously. He fell down on the ground. In Gethsemane he fell down on his face, afraid, wanting to be let off! He falls under the cross, an example to the timid, the frightened, the weak.

Jesus falls *under the cross,* the cross made of wood, matter, made of a tree that he made himself without effort, a cross, a thing made by man. He wants to show us what our cross is: material things, man-made difficulties. When I can't stand up to things, he wants to show me something: that I am not greater than Christ, that no one is, that I must despise no one who falls under the cross, that I must be patient with myself.

And when I fall, the first time especially, what a light I have on myself! I thought I was strong, that gross temptation would not move me, that I would be faithful in all sorts of environment. I am down—in the dirt—I know myself now! But I know God, too, as I did not before, now I know the radiance of the shadowless light, I know now what sin is.

Before, I scratched at my soul for scruples, concentrated on myself, my "perfection"—now I am in the dirt and I know, and I know what it is to be forgiven, the goodness of God, the mercy of God, God's love!—what can I do but get up, fix my gaze on God and rejoice in him?

SIMON OF CYRENE

He was forced to help Christ.
He thought that Christ was just a poor criminal.
He did not realize the joy that was forced upon him.

After, when he understood ?—I cannot guess the heaven of that!

We are forced to help Christ, to carry his cross with him.

We think that he is a tiresome relation, or some bore who wants too much attention but cannot be escaped, a fellow-worker who makes endless demands on our sympathy, or a beggar whom we would prefer to pass but somehow cannot.

Or it may be the whole circumstance of our life is a cross, forced on us. We think we chose wrongly. Our job is uncongenial, we could do wonders in another kind of job, we have no scope, it is all wrong, a ghastly mistake!

But it isn't wrong. In the beginning we are forced to share his burden, but it is the only way for us. If we had chosen, we might have missed his cross—we might not have had the chance to help Christ in his passion. There is no irony in life, only God's mercy.

And when we realize! When we are no longer forced, but every day gladly comfort Christ in all those trying people, gladly share his burden in the world—I cannot guess the heaven of that. I can only be grateful that I too am forced to take up the cross of Christ and may one day understand.

Jesus meets his mother. His sorrow deeper because of their love. Because of her grief, his grief is limitless. He could have spared himself this. But he has never spared himself the inevitable deepening of every experience to those who love, who have the courage to face that responsibility without flinching. He has taught love, he is love, he will not shut his eyes to his mother, will not spare his heart from her. He will not send her away, she meets him only to go with him, to be with him to the very end.

He meets the women of Jerusalem. He warns them, he does not accept their pity. He warns all pious women, who meditate on the passion, weep before crucifixes of ivory, but not over the Crucified in their souls. Those who have no tears for the children who are heirs to the abuses and cruelties of generations of greed, culminating in the big cities we know, with their slums, their worldliness, their sweated labour, their vice. Those who have no tears for the homeless, the insane, the criminal, the Spanish refugees, the martyrs of Russia, the hunted Jews, the miners underground in the dark, the unemployed! "Weep not for Me, but for yourselves and for your children!"

He meets Veronica. His image on her veil; a bruised face, the beauty hidden by suffering; how like him to leave only that image of his face to the world!

The veil, white linen, the simple, unfolded quality, the only thing that can receive his impress. The courage of the woman! Facing his misery, touching it, opposing the crowd, ignoring public opinion, the reality of her love!

And now, on the face of the world, not just dirt and misery, but the face of Christ hidden under what we see. Only strong love, courageous, individual, pure, can approach the sin, the misery and pain, that covers the face of Christ now.

Christ on the Cross

THEN

Christ is alone on the cross; they have stripped him of his garments. The crowds pass by, they do not recognize who this poor man is; He is naked, shamed, counted with thieves; they pass him by.

His mother must suffer because of him. He cannot comfort her. He must leave her to his friend, it is because He loves her that she must suffer.

It seems such a failure! Even God is mocked because of his supreme sacrifice to God. His very faith in his Father is used to deny God.

Love holds him to the cross, he is on the cross because he *is* love, redeeming, but they will only believe in him if he comes down from the cross!

NOW

Christ is alone on the cross. Every day I pass him in the crowd. I do not recognize him in every poor man. He is poor, humiliated, suspect for his misery. I pass him by.

To follow him always, without compromise, I must sometimes grieve some who love me. Sometimes my own parents. "Son, why hast Thou done so to us?"

When I try to keep the laws of the Church, which conflict with public opinion God is the more abused. "A good God would not ask that of you."

His love has turned the results of sin to a cross that redeems. It is love that keeps him suffering in men, but they will only

Lest even his love should fail, he has nailed himself to the cross, he has made sure of his loyalty to us! Lest his humanity fail he has made sure of having to go on, to stay there, to suffer our blindness, his mother's grief, the shame, the failure, the loss of God. Perfect love has driven nails into his hands and feet that he may not fail me! "Father, not my will but Thy will be done." He has fastened himself with nails, that when things fail him, he may not fail.

believe in him if he will end suffering.

I who am wholly human, afraid, unfaithful, must yet be one with him. Can *I* remain faithful, when I am misunderstood, when I must give pain where I love, when I am shamed by my sins, when all that I attempt for him fails? When I experience, as I must, identified with Christ, the loss of the sense of God? When I fail myself? I can only pledge my love and make my promise nails to hold me when there is nothing else.

When it is consummated, completed, he is laid in Mary's arms. He is at peace now! The pain she gave to him in Bethlehem is at last used up. Now she holds him in her arms, in peace. Only heaven waits for him now.

We must each give birth to Christ in our life, from the hour when he is born in us we must let him go through his passion in us; but when it is consummated, when we have given all we have, soul and body to him, we shall know what it is to receive him into our hearts at peace, to hold him in silence and stillness, waiting only for heaven.

He is laid in the tomb, and the tomb is not only in the rock, it is every city in the world, every town and village and home, it is every human heart. Christ lies in the tomb now, a few like the ardent boy John and the passionate lover Magdalene seek him in the cities, in the hearts of men. The crowds still pass by. Christ is in the tomb awaiting the Easter of the world, his resurrection in us.

> Christ,
> nailed to the cross,
> nailed there by your own will,
> for us and with us,
> nail us to the cross,
> for you and with you.
> Make the ardour and the ardent promises of
>   our youth sincere,
> sincere enough to nail and hold us
> and keep us faithful to you.
> When our youth passes and with it our
>   dreams and the ardour of youth

let us remember our promises

and renew them with the will and the real
    love

that nailed you to the cross.

When we die

let these nails be in our hands and our feet.

When we rise again,

let us rise again with the burning stars of your
    wounds

shining upon us for ever.

Amen.

FOUR

THE DEFENCES OF THE MIND

We have been at war for nearly two years. Tremendous things have happened. Our old habits and routines have been swept away, and with them security. We have to adjust ourselves not only to new ways of living, to blackouts and ration cards and the rest, but to the presence of fear. He would be less than human—not more—who did not experience anxiety and fear. People who never did a hand's turn before, find themselves hard at work from morning till night, sometimes from night till morning, while many who never stopped working are forced to be idle. Amusements have been reduced to nearly nothing. People who thought to remain inseparable are parted, and unbelievably incongruous groups work in complete harmony together. Those whose leg we thought might wither with disuse, those who could not imagine life without a car, are by curious irony pedalling away on bicycles, while others have at last learnt to walk. Children who were born to the London slums have suddenly awoken to the singing of birds over green pastures. Grandmothers have become fire-fighters. These are but a few of the things that have happened in this short space, which seems to most of us like many years.

Things have happened which have changed the course of our lives for ever. Of course I do not mean that after the war we shall go on doing the things we are doing now. I do not mean, to give an example, that large numbers of people will walk about the streets in tin hats for ever. Oh no, just now the world is metaphorically mad, standing on its head, forced to be mad, that it may *be* at all; but after the war we shall stand on our feet and take off our tin hats.

After the war what will have happened to the mind under the tin hat?

The mind of man is assailed as never before, and on the whole it is without defences. The most urgent and most vital thing now is to build defences for the mind.

While we have made most elaborate and intensive preparations for the defences of the body, the mind, which is so much more vulnerable and in such immediate danger, is so far without defences.

Now is the time to prepare defences for the mind.

Against what enemies are we to build our defences?

The first is *fear,* fear for ourselves, fear for those we love—and fear breeds hatred. United to rumour, gossip and propaganda it breeds hatred almost before we know it. Fear and hatred are the most terrible enemies of the war.

Next, there is—at all events for war workers—*lack of privacy.* Apart from the real crucifixion that this is to sensitive people, it is the cause of a lot of repressions. We feel that we must on no account show feeling before others. Doctors tell us that as much neurasthenia was caused through this kind of repression as through real shock in the first World War.

Those who are in danger zones have to prepare against severe *physical shock* and *nervous tension.* Those working for national service in danger zones must add to those one of the most difficult things to manage, *want of sleep,* and the increasing domination of physical necessities brought about by a continual demand on our energy and later accentuated by poverty.

A further danger for many is the *loss of individuality;* when our day is mapped and disciplined and encircled within narrow limits, when we are, as we must be during the war, parts of a machine, the power of thinking can easily die.

At present it is unnecessary to speak of any other of our mental assailments. War, though it strikes a spark of chivalry from the heart, is on the whole dehumanizing, and the reason we need the defences of the mind is that, whatever comes, we may remain in the truest sense human; preserving not only the life of the body, but that life which illuminates and heals the world, the life of which Christ said: "I have come that they may have life, and may have it more abundantly."

When I first thought that the circumstances were such that we really had got actually to plan out defences for our mind, I wondered how they could be planned. People react so differently, and danger lurks on so many sides. It is clear that our defences must be those which will be proof against any circumstances, and some of them ones which everyone can use.

The gospel for the 14th Sunday after Pentecost gave me a clue. It was not by chance that on the day on which war broke out the gospel was taken from the Sermon on the Mount. The 14th Sunday gospel says: trust God, be not solicitous for your life, for your clothes or your food, be care-free, your heavenly Father will care for you, and if you want proof of God's love, then look round you at the things he has made, and do not be content only to look, but meditate upon them and on the mysteries they hint at—"Consider the lilies of the field," says Our Lord, "consider the birds of the air." On the day war is declared, knowing all the difficulties in our way, Christ repeats the gentlest of his words, which are also the most uncompromising, which have been the most consistently avoided ever since he uttered them, by all but the saints.

For those words beginning: "No man can serve two masters," and ending, "Seek ye therefore first the kingdom of God and his justice . . ." are *Christ's peace plan,* and his peace plan is not to be delayed, it is to begin now. For no peace on earth will be other than a mockery unless in the hearts of Christians peace comes now.

For my part, I can lift my heart, when I think that on that black day, this imperious love of Christ uttered itself wherever Mass was offered; that on German and Dutch and Polish and French and English souls fell this blessed rain of mercy; it gives me to hope, indeed to trust, that whatever we are asked to suffer will be worthwhile, that it will be a sowing of seed.

On hearing those words at the time, I thought that first of all our whole attitude to suffering must be faced. So long as we evade what we are to face, other things that could help, such as music, poetry and so on, are only escapes, they do not help; but before we can think quietly and peacefully enough to form a clear idea concerning the meaning of suffering and of war in particular, we have to recover from the first shock of war.

We have been shocked; to deny that is to deny that we are human. Shock makes it very hard to think, very hard to begin to concentrate again, and so we cannot even begin to formulate a quiet strong attitude to suffering until our minds are healed. Besides, uprooted as we are, with new routines, concentration is even more difficult. What, then, is to be said for my first defence, "A clearly-defined attitude to war"? Simply, that it has made me realize that that is not the first, but the second, defence. *The first is prayer.*

Prayer is a healing thing, and our first defence must begin to heal even while it fortifies us, and it must be the reserve on which we can draw over and over again.

Prayer alone can teach us to concentrate again, can lead us to absolute trust in God, and make our minds ready for other essential things spoken of in that gospel; for the contemplation (not mere observation) of beauty.

PRAYER, THE FIRST DEFENCE

First of all, it was Christ's defence. "Being in an agony, he prayed the more." And many times he went alone by himself to pray. Very few of us can go alone by ourselves to pray now. That is a great difficulty, especially for those on National Service, we are hardly ever alone, day or night. Another difficulty is the dislocation of time. An old lady whom I know, always dined through her long life on bread and milk. "You see, dear," she said, "if I did not, I should forget my night prayers." So strong is the habit-forming power of the nursery routine! But our routine has been swept away too. Gradually we shall get used to new conditions, and form mental habits in them; actually, we are forming these habits now, that is why prayer must be woven into them *now* or it never will be.

But when can we pray, and where?—All the time, and everywhere. As Our Lord says, pray without ceasing. If this does not come naturally, it must be learnt. There are ways of learning it.

First of all, we can be rid of some false ideas on prayer. Many have been taught that unless you are on your knees, and unless you say a lot, you are not praying; that you pray with words and thoughts only. This is wrong, prayer is raising the heart and mind to God. You pray, when you pray well, with your body, with your hands and feet and head and heart, your ribs pray, your ears pray, your eyes pray.

Do you think that because Christ was not on his knees at the Last Supper, he did not pray? Do you not realize that when he was on the cross, his hands and feet prayed?

So first of all realize that your body—offered in sacrifice as the Host in the Mass is offered in sacrifice—is praying. If you do realize this, every call on your energy, every ache in your limbs, even every yawn you stifle, will remind you of God, and gradually the offering of self, in your work, through your body, will become deliberate, countless times in the day you will become conscious of God. If your head aches, you offer it to him, you become conscious of him, and so it goes on.

The best offering, that is, the best form of offering, I know, is just to say the one word "God" and let it pervade you; but if you are going to use that word take five, or even three, minutes a day to think about God; think that you are only alive because at this moment he wills you to be alive, because at this moment his love creates you, wills you to be: think that his eyes watch you, his hands are around you, they shelter your life as a flame is sheltered in the storm.

So—when you feel weary, and say "God"—it will be more than saying a word, it will be letting yourself rest in his infinite love, easing the tension and letting yourself float upstream to him: trust will grow, peace will grow. Above all, the habit of prayer will grow, and the harder days will be the days most woven through with the light of God. To say the name of God in this way does weave our days with light, just as the world is woven through, with the sun's rays at twilight, and because of the darkness we are able to see the warmth and beauty of the light.

This offering of self through the body has reminded me during the night of the Agony in the Garden, when Our Lord came and found his apostles asleep—well, once or twice he has found me asleep on night duty, but here is a literal chance of just praying by staying awake to atone for sin.

Another way, or perhaps a variation of that way, is to take one prayer like the "Our Father" and weave it through the day. Choose, not a special time for meditation, but a special job, one you do every day; if, for example, you are a nurse, while you are sterilizing is a good time, and there meditate on the meaning of one phrase of the "Our Father"—if you like, one word: "Our"—whose Father? Everyone's, Germans', Englishmen's, Father of my enemy, therefore they are my brothers, I have no enemy; I pray also for them. "Our Father"—whose Father? Father of those I love and tremble for, therefore loving them more than I do, caring for them more than I can—and so on. Meditate in this way, not trying to cover the whole prayer in a day, but going slowly and making it real and alive to you.

Then, take all day to say the "Our Father," once, just go on, from phrase to phrase, not trying now to mean anything, trying only to lull your thoughts to a rhythm of prayer, which will run all through the day and become habit, but a habit which has thought behind it, so that in an emergency the words will come to your mind mechanically, and not only will they calm you, like the familiar voice of your mother, but their meaning, stored in your heart, will fill you then.

Lately I learnt something which made me understand as never before the beauty of the habit of prayer. A Jew was telling me that he so wished in these days that he had faith; he was building a sandbag wall and foolishly I had dropped my crucifix into it; he insisted on undoing his wall and getting it for me. He was a stranger, and I did not know him; he was standing holding my crucifix, looking at it with a puzzled wistfulness. "Of course," he said, "I'm a Jew, my mother was a good Jewess, I never learnt nothing about Christ, we don't bother to, but I did learn to say my prayers day and night, and I wish I 'ad kept it up."

"What did you say?" I asked.

"Well, the morning ones was long, but the night was short; all us little Jew kids said it as we fell asleep."

"What was it?"

"Well, Miss, it went like this: 'Father, into Thy hands I commend my spirit.' It's what mothers teached little

Jewish boys ever since the world began, they do say, they tells 'em to say it just before they falls asleep."

I don't need even to comment on that!

"LORD, TEACH US TO PRAY"

His response to that plea is far more than a form of words. Like all his teaching, it is an answer to all fundamental questions, for all times, our own included. He gives us an attitude of mind to God and man, teaches us what trust means, and on what conditions God will accept our adoration. Every word repays meditation, and the more real the prayer becomes, the more full of meaning for us, the more it will give us light and courage when we use it: even—or perhaps especially—when because of stress we say it mechanically.

OUR

Christ always stresses "our" and "we," "ours" and "us," never "I" and "me" and "mine." Everything is ours, the burden of sin, the suffering of the world, the responsibility of facing it, the work of the world; and ours too the glory of the saints, the graces of all the faithful, the ardours of the holy souls. We are all one, we cannot be "neutral" and human; we are all one in Christ.

This attitude of "our" and "ours," Christ's attitude, cuts out all pharisaism, all isolation, all that aloofness which dares to exhort others to repent. There is no "them" or "they" for Christians; if we see guilt, the guilt is ours, the duty of reparation is ours, the bearing of the burden is ours. The present agony of the world is ours; if we are Christians we are bound to enter into it, to accept our responsibility for it, to share to the full the work of defending, healing, saving, through hard work, through true contrition, through deep humility, through service.

OUR FATHER

Our oneness, our kinship, everything that binds us, depends on this, that God is our Father. This decides our attitude to our enemies. The enemy may kill our brothers, but he is himself our brother. A hard fact? Yes, it may be, but deny it and we deny God's Fatherhood.

Christ is brother to us all, God is Father to us all. Our Father loves all his children and grieves over all their suffering, all their sins, all their blindness, all their folly. Think of all Christ says of our Father: the story of the prodigal son; the gifts of sun and rain to the just and the unjust alike; how often he stresses that none on this earth are exempt from his bounty, that we may not sort out, separate, good from bad—let the cockle grow—God is the Father, intent upon saving everyone. God is the Father of sinners as well as saints. He is Father of the poor,

Father of the afflicted, he expects us to treat them all as brothers, as his dear children.

Having one common Father we have certain fundamental things in common; all want happiness, no matter how different the conception of it; all desire to love; all have some family resemblance to God, our Creator, our Father. Therefore this Fatherhood is our one hope for peace, for the coming of God's kingdom, for all else that we pray for in the "Our Father."

WHO ART IN HEAVEN

Why does Christ stress this? God is everywhere: yes, but how dim faith is, what a remote idea heaven is, in the modern world! True, if we knew God here as we could know God here, we should touch heaven now, even in this world as it is. But we don't know God as we ought to, and we have made a mess of our life here, we have to remind ourselves that heaven actually exists, death is not the end of life, but the beginning; God is in heaven, changeless, at peace, eternal; in him there is illimitable joy for us.

HALLOWED BE THY NAME

There are several meanings: one, "May Your name be praised, may You be adored," another, "May Your name be made holy."

All Christ's mind was always concentrated on adoration of his Father. How little is he adored now? Adoration is a necessity to man, his heart must adore or die; men fallen away from God adore—or idolize—power, State, machinery, anything that seems bigger than themselves, to combine mystery with might.

The Christian must adore God, with words and deeds, through the Mass, through the sacrifice of himself in union with the Mass, through the absolute dedication of his whole heart. Even through this, the other meaning, "May Your name be made holy," becomes clear: through the presence of Christ in men, God is glorified, his holiness is seen, his name is honoured. It is the same as the son of a noble house making a glorious name yet more glorious by the integrity of his own life. He is, we say, "worthy of his father's blood." But such a thing between Our heavenly Father and ourselves can only happen through Christ acting in us.

"Let your works so shine before men that they may glorify your Father who is in heaven."

This prayer: "Hallowed be thy name" prays that God be adored, that he be adored by Christ in us, prays that Christ be in us, and so may give glory to God through our lives.

THY KINGDOM COME

This touches the whole of our life; what is this kingdom of God's? Is it a material kingdom, in which the good prosper, a kingdom which will be visible on earth and will defeat the tyrannies that we are fighting?

The apostles thought it would be a material kingdom, they seemed to hope so; all the Jews thought so, they did not seem able to conceive of anything else. Many, many people now cannot conceive of anything else. Christ gave the answer: "My kingdom is not of this world"; "The kingdom of heaven is within you." And facing Pilate, affirming his own kingship to him, he said that if he were an earthly king he would call on men and angels to defend him.

To-day, Christ, the innocent Man, the Man of humility and love, could summon angels to defend his life in his members. He could turn the stones into legions and he could take the world. But the kingdom is in man's heart; the patient soul who rules her own heart with an ordered tenderness, pity and kindness, the mind that keeps the poetry of life in flower, even now, that is the soul who possesses the kingdom of God. But if most Christians, most people, had this inward kingdom, cherished it, then there would be also a visible kingdom, not a kingdom based on materialism, not a kingdom based on power, but conditions of life based on simplicity, brotherly love and sacrifice, which would make it impossible to go to war, impossible to have slums or destitution, impossible to have enmity between countries, classes or individuals.

Christ, claiming the kingdom, proclaiming himself King, did not resist evil; he suffered for it. His crown was a crown of thorns and the shedding of his blood was the sowing of his seed.

Now, to-day, but for Christ, we could logically despair. "What hope," we could say, "of reforms now? How build up any conditions in which all men can live in the most austere happiness? Everything is being destroyed, all the brain, the science, the strength of man is being used for destruction." If the kingdom were a material one, then hope would be absurd. But we are told to pray it may come, and come it can and will, first in heart after heart, mind after mind, coming as the growth of love, as a light flooding the mind, until, aware of the wonder of it, we shall dare in Christ's name either to live for it or to die for it, knowing that not one jot of suffering can be wasted or miss the mark, since all of it is his sacrifice.

THY WILL BE DONE ON EARTH AS IT IS IN HEAVEN

What is his will? His will is love: he wills that men shall live lives which through love are good and happy, that in each life he shall come to flower, and as it happens with natural flowers, when he flowers in men they die to themselves and give his life. All loveliness flowers only to spend itself in giving life. God's will is not our death, but our life, but since we have sinned and Christ has redeemed us, even death has been changed. It is no longer only a punishment, it is also a redemption, it can also give life.

"Thy will be done," Christ said, accepting his passion after the bitter struggle in Gethsemane; so God, who desires us to live and sent Christ to make our life increase, let him die. Why? In order that even death, the final result of evil, should be changed by love into life; it should be the door of resurrection and the sowing of the seed of the soul's life.

"Thy will be done" means, let Your love flower and blossom with life, and since we have sinned, let even our bitter sorrows, not willed by God, give life through his mercy; thus, trusting him, we can trust that through whatever happens to us his will will be done.

Give Us This Day Our Daily Bread

Here indeed is the simplest of all these petitions. First it prays for the blessed sacrament, and secondly for food for our bodies. Our daily bread is threatened, but it has always come from God's hand. Man can manufacture death, man can mend and stimulate life, man can speed and increase his crops; but life itself, the life in the seed, the life in the wheat, that God alone can give. With all the bitter death he deals, man does not yet know what life is. Give us our Bread, our Christ, our Food, our Life.

FORGIVE US OUR TRESPASSES AS WE FORGIVE THEM THAT TRESPASS AGAINST US

That is stern and merciful. God wills that we forgive, and he forgives exactly as we forgive. If we forgive completely, so will he; if with reserves, so will he; if not at all, he will not forgive. If we do not forgive, we are asking to be judged; we dare not say this prayer with a hard heart. But if we forgive wholly, we have won our Father's absolute pardon; it is a petition which can be an absolution in itself.

LEAD US NOT INTO TEMPTATION BUT DELIVER US FROM EVIL

It is puzzling, this. It can mean, let Your will be done, Your kingdom come, Your love prevail, in order that we may not be forced to live under conditions which make it inhumanly difficult to keep God's law. It may mean, since the evil has already come upon us, deliver us, bring us out of this dark night to that dawn we long for, that new light of Your eternal love, in which we shall see the ruin of so much that we cherished, but in which our own spirits shall be washed pure of so much dross.

It can mean, deliver our country. It can mean, deliver us from our self. It may mean something different for everyone who utters it. Perhaps Christ, who loves us to try to unravel his lovely secrets, who himself has a lover's way of playing hide-and-seek with us, has deliberately left it a little obscure. But in general it means, bring us out, deliver us from everything that is not You, do not let our sins and our sorrows crush us now and cause us to despair, but draw us up out of them and into Your presence, as the sun draws up the flowers from the dark swarming earth to the light of the day.

> Our Father, who art in heaven,
>
> Hallowed be thy name,
>
> Thy kingdom come,
>
> Thy will be done on earth as it is in heaven:
>
> Give us this day our daily bread,
>
> And forgive us our trespasses as we forgive
> them that trespass
> against us,
>
> And lead us not into temptation but deliver
> us from evil.
>
> Amen.

"DO THIS IN REMEMBRANCE OF ME"

To those who are used to daily Mass there is no privation more terrible than that of having to do without it. This is not because of any spiritual consolation that they have known, for usually those who go to Mass daily suffer torturing distractions and a kind of numbness of spirit which makes it a hard, and not always successful, act of will to concentrate on the prayers in the missal at all.

If "spiritual sweetness" were the object of the soul, and daily distress through aridity its actual portion, surely the sudden ceasing of Mass would be a relief? The proof that the blessed sacrament is in very truth our food and strength is that, no matter how little sensible comfort we have in it, no matter how little we realize what it does for us, let it be taken away and we immediately feel our weakness, we have a true famine of the soul, which nothing else can satisfy. It is really like ordinary bread, we do not realize what bread is to us until we have to do without it, but then we know well enough that it is indeed life to us.

There are many people to-day who are in fact having to do without daily Mass. War service often imposes this on them, and they accept it, because their war service is in itself their Christianity now, and it is the fruit of many Masses.

The time may come, and come soon, when for an indefinite time war conditions make it more and more difficult for any of us to hear Mass at all, even on Sundays, and we shall all understand why our forefathers in the days of persecution were willing to give up everything— property, honours, freedom, even life itself—for the glory of being present even at one Mass.

Suppose such conditions do come, is there any way in which we can prepare for them and make it easier for us to suffer them? There is; and if after making this preparation we are spared the necessity of using it, we can be sure that all the same our lives will be richer as a result of it.

The first part of this preparation is to make ourselves more and more deeply aware of what the Mass is. It is not only a set of old, beautiful prayers offered each morning in our parish church. No, it is a sacrifice which is always being offered and in which we can always take part at any time and anywhere. It is not a sacrifice offered by a priest in which our part is merely that of a devout audience. It is a sacrifice which gathers every circumstance of our life to itself and is the very core of our being.

We need not fear that because we might not be able to be actually present at Mass, Mass is no longer celebrated. Mass will always be celebrated, while the world lasts. It is the sacrifice foretold by the prophets, which must always be offered from sunrise to sunset, a promise to us which cannot and will not be broken.

To keep this promise of God's, his saints have given their lives over and over again, and Mass has been celebrated in many strange and secret places, beginning in the borrowed room where Christ instituted the sacrament of his body, and afterwards in the Catacombs, where the early Christians were forced, as we are forced to-day, to tunnel under the ground for safety. Wherever the Church has been persecuted, Mass has again been offered in the borrowed rooms of friends of Christ; many an English home has been hallowed by it, and in the latter years it has been offered in more and more unlikely places. In the desert by the lonely and heroic Charles de Foucauld, in the forests of Siberia by the Russian prisoners, and—because the astonishing humility of Our Lord has not altered since he came, in a poor stable—in little tin huts and tea-shops and barns in this country, which still denies Christ his cathedrals.

It will continue. There will always be those who will offer Mass, and Christ will always, with his divine ingenuity and lowliness, find a place to come to for us.

This being so, we can always, though possibly from a distance, unite ourselves with the Mass that is being offered. There is never a moment when the Host is not being offered up for us, never a moment when we cannot lift ourselves up with Christ crucified.

To do this, to unite ourselves with the Mass, which, though unseen, is really happening, we need to be very familiar with what happens at Mass. Just the broad essentials.

First there is great sorrow for sin, bowing down low, confessing that we are sinners, asking God's pardon for the world, and no one should begin to think of joining in the Mass without this sorrow and this humility. Next there is the statement of faith, the gospels, the creed; and our faith is the one thing that we can take pride in, it is our sword and our light. Then there is the Offertory, the offering of bread and wine to God, to be changed into the Host. Then the Consecration, when the miracle has happened and Christ is there on the cross, adoring for us, atoning for us, pleading for us. And afterwards the communion, when he is united to us in a oneness for which we have no parallel in any human love, though it includes them all.

Keeping these elementary facts of the Mass in mind we can, without a missal, join in any Mass going on, and be really present to Christ on some secret altar. And such a habit can weave itself all through our life and absorb all our life into itself.

First, the Confiteor: we can start our spiritual Mass by recalling the great burden of sin laid upon us all, and though we may be in a crowd, or at some duty, unable to bow down our heads and strike our breasts, we can bow our minds and humble our hearts by inwardly accepting from God all our own personal grief and hardship caused by the war, as our just due for our share in the world's sin. We can check our passing rebellion and recall our littleness, and bow down before God.

We can join in the gospel and the creed by recalling the mysteries of our faith and professing them to God. We need to remind ourselves of them constantly, and to take the wonderful comfort in them—for example, the communion of saints and the resurrection of the body! Everyone knows the creed, and everyone can repeat it in his or her own mind. At this point, too, we can offer to God our mind and heart and lips, and pray, as we do at Mass, to have our tongues touched with fire in order to be able to speak of our faith well.

Then the Offertory. We can now offer to God all that we are and all that we are enduring, and even all the joys we have or must forgo:—our life, literally, our bodies and souls, our thoughts and work, everything we have. We have got to suffer anyway, and this offertory can make our suffering what the fire is to the Host, something that sifts and purifies us and makes us ready to ask Our Lord to change us into himself.

When we have made our offertory, we come to the Consecration; and now we can lift the Christ crucified in our own lives in union with the Host now being elevated, to adore God, to plead for everyone, to atone for everything. And finally, we can make our spiritual communion, which everyone knows how to do.

Briefly, using all our circumstances and all our will, this would be the order of such a spiritual Mass (and we shall really be united to all the Masses being celebrated on earth):

(1) *Sorrow for sin.* I accept all as just. I offer all in atonement. I acknowledge that I am not fit to approach God. I ask his pardon.

(2) *Offering.* I offer myself, and all that I have, to God.

(3) *Consecration.* God accepts my offering, and changes it into Christ.

(4) *Communion.* I gave myself to God; now, in Christ, he gives himself back to me.

All this can be done without any words at all, but it will help still more to know, and to say in one's own head, at least the principal prayers in the missal, because they are full of strength and beauty and would keep alive in us the love and understanding of the Mass during even very long privation.

For so long as we cherish the Mass in our hearts, the flame of faith will burn brightly in us, and each time we join in the Mass, though not bodily present, we shall receive all the illimitable grace of the Mass, and shall have the power of Christ to adore and to atone, and all that we have to suffer and to offer, all that we are, will be changed into him and will be one thing with the redeeming sacrifice of his triumphant love.

RELAXATION

Just now the cat is lying by the fire in a state of complete abandonment. He knows nothing and cares nothing for war, he has unlimited confidence in me, he is sure that I shall always feed him and warm him and house him. It is humiliating to be trusted like that, and though his very trust will make me do my utmost not to let him down, his well-being is a source of anxiety. However, he does not know that; he thinks that I am all powerful, and so he is perfectly relaxed. He can be the opposite. If he scents danger he bristles, his hair stands on end, his backbone juts, his eyes squint, and he walks with stiff legs on the tips of his nails.

We have a lot to learn from the cat. At present we are bristling, squinting, stiffening even more than usual, but we are always too tense, even in times of peace.

There can hardly be anyone who has not read articles, or whole books, on the subject of relaxing a nervous tension, or who, at least, has not listened to long dissertations on the subject. Consequently, most people know that if they suffer from nervous tension it is a good plan to lie on the floor, sofa, or bed, and let themselves go. Somewhat elaborate instructions are usually given about how to do it; some experts favour relaxing each limb in turn, others suggest restful little thoughts as such: "imagine yourself to be falling through the bed!"

Those who have tried it know that the first thing they discover is that they are in fact more tense than they thought, that it is, at first anyhow, a positively exhausting process: they become conscious of the tautness of different muscles and the consciousness is positively painful. Moreover, when one has succeeded in relaxing one part, another is all the more felt; for example, if I unscrew my eyes and unclench my teeth I become nose-conscious or flap my ears. The books promise that if I go on patiently I shall finally triumph, but I doubt this, for though I do in fact realize that nervous tension is very destructive and requires some kind of self-treatment, I do not believe in the effectiveness of any treatment which begins from outside. I do not think our bodies are tense because of outside things, but because the soul, which never for a moment ceases to act on the body, is tense.

What causes tension, nervous and spiritual? That is a pertinent question, and the answer may hold the secret of a cure. It is anxiety.

The symptoms of anxiety are scruples, exaggerated sense of responsibility, a continual feeling of guilt or uneasiness, etc. Those who suffer seriously from these really distressing maladies are anxious in case they fail to satisfy their own ideal of themselves, they attach much too much importance to their own perfection and their own work, they do not attach half enough importance to God's love and God's will.

A very good exercise for those who are suffering in this way is to kneel down night after night and just say one brief, simple and true prayer: "Dear God, my name is mud!"

But during war, there are more causes of real anxiety, they are patent to us all.

My cat (I can't neglect him for long, as to-day he is my spiritual director!) is a tabby. Just now he was in the garden when a black cat came loping along the garden wall, a very unpleasant fellow, I must admit, definitely marked by the underworld; my tabby became very anxious. He rushed to the window, his pink mouth wide open, his face raddled with fear. I let him in, and no sooner had he jumped on my lap than he relaxed, he went limp, not with fear, but happily, deliciously limp, and indicated by various signs known to me that he wanted his ears scratched—that done, he went to sleep.

This is a lesson in prayer. There are many ways of prayer: to "lift up the heart and mind to God" covers a huge range. There is prayer like that of Moses, when he lifted his arms and held them up, straining and agonizing, before God; there is the prayer which Christ describes in one of his parables, which could be called "the prayer of importunity," a continual hammering and beating on the door of heaven until we get what we want; and many others. But now, with such great anxiety pressing upon us, the prayer in which we can relax is surely among the most creative.

We certainly should pray all the time, praying with our hands, our bodies, our will, our acts, but in order to delight God and to build up the peace of our souls, besides the prayer in which we offer ourselves to God should be the prayer in which we let God give himself to us. We should learn to receive the love of God in silence and joy—that is what is meant by relaxing.

There should be, even in the busiest day, a few moments when we can close our eyes and let God possess us. He is always present, always giving us life, always round us and in us, like the air we breathe; there should be moments at least when we become more conscious of his presence: when we become conscious of it as the only reality, the only thing that will last for ever.

But it is not so easy as it sounds to do this. We are too tense, we do not know how to use those blessed moments when we are alone, or in the presence of the blessed sacrament. Our mistake is that we make an effort, we become anxious, we think that if we fail to concentrate we fail to pray; between distraction and weariness the moment is wasted.

What is to be done? I ought to be able to treat God as my cat treats me; only, whereas my cat is deluded about my omnipotence, I am right about God's.

But there is something for me to fear, to be anxious about, something equivalent in my life to the black underworld Tom in my cat's life. I ought to be able to relax, however, to stop being afraid, the moment I realize that I am in God's presence. I ought to want him to make his love known to me; my prayer should just be accepting, trusting, and even in a sense sleeping, in that love. If it were possible for me to cease absolutely from fear and anxiety even once a day for ten minutes, or several times a day for two minutes, I should very soon find that I did not suffer from nervous tension any more.

There are ways of learning to relax, and all prayer is stronger if we can. One way is to learn to trust God all the time, to practise trust in everyday life.

I do not hesitate to say that first of all we must learn to trust God, because this is only what Christ taught. He told us to live in the present; his whole teaching stresses that idea. "Take no thought of the morrow, sufficient unto the day is the evil thereof." He tells us not to save up, or make any provision for the future, to live in the moment. But we seldom do so, we seldom consciously rejoice because to-day is a soft blue day of mist and sunlight and we are still with those dear to us, clothed, fed and under our own roof, No, we grieve because of what to-morrow may bring. To live in the day is the beginning of being care-free.

But trust does not mean believing that God will spare us from suffering. It means believing that if God lets us suffer it is because there is good for us in it, it is always an expression of his love, and even out of sin, which is evil in itself, good can come. There is no beauty in the boast of virtue, even if it be true, but tears of contrition make the angels glad; they are beautiful in the eyes of God and men, yet there could be no sorrow for sin, without sin.

To trust God means that we must know that whatever comes to us comes from his hand. If we do not see that sorrow comes from his hand and cannot get the comfort of his love from it, it may be because we do not acknowledge our joys as his gifts. If we felt grateful for our food, for the sunlight, for our work, our homes, for those we love, if we were conscious that these were all given by God, we should have formed a clear enough idea of his love to know him; we should know him well enough to know, because we know him, that he does not want us to suffer, but allows it because there is good for us in it. To resist, to be bitter, to say it is no use, all increases the pain. To accept it gratefully from God eases the pain. Christ says: "Take no thought of to-morrow." He also says: "Take up your cross daily." There is no need, in accepting sorrow, to look ahead, to imagine to-morrow, to ask for more or less, but just as we receive our joy day by day, so can we receive our sorrow day by day, and it will be measured day by day, by the love of God and our own littleness.

The saints do not *accept* suffering, they rejoice in it. It is doubtful if any others but saints could do that, but the practice of trust may be the beginning

To look for God's gift in the moment is the way to learn to trust. It is better to begin by knowing him through the happy things, to guess his beauty from the colour in a rose, the fire in the stars, the purity in a bowl of water; to guess his providence in the food we eat and the clothes we wear and the bed we lie in; dimly to discern his love in the kindness of friends and the tenderness of those who love us. The smaller the things are for which we thank God the more we learn of him; we learn that he is interested in the details of our life and knows the exact mentality of each one of us. He will make himself known to one through mental conflict, but to another through a bird's nest and the fragile miracles of life that we call bird's eggs. A mystic in the Middle Ages learnt his glory from an acorn, and I can learn a lot from the cat. This is not because we discover for ourselves what ways we can find God, it is because God, Who knows the fine shades of our mind and heart, sends his love to us in the way that he knows we can receive it, through this friend, through that flower, and so on. It must, then, be clear that so loving a Father, a Father Who will even make daisies, insects, tree frogs and dewdrops to humour and coax his children, Who knows them so well and loves them so well, can also be trusted when he gives us sorrow.

We shall have sorrow. Trust means, no cowardly shrinking from truth; but the sorrow will be chosen by God for each of us, and it will come to each of us in the measure and in the kind which God, knowing us, chooses for us and for our good.

Now is there a way in which a busy person could practise this growing trust, without having to meditate all day long?—Yes, it is very simple. Make a mental picture of two huge giving hands, God's hands, and every so often in the day or night, stop for a moment and think: "At this moment, God is handing me all I have, my life—" and so on, mentioning all that you are conscious of. It may be at some moments you will realize what a lot of obvious good God is giving you still, at other times it will help you to understand that the trials you suffer also come from his hands.

Real trust believes Our Lord, who started the Sermon on the Mount by saying that suffering is a blessed thing: Blessed are the poor, the mourners, the persecuted.

RHYTHMIC PRAYER

All that has been said on prayer in the previous articles leads quite naturally to the subject of rhythmic prayer. The official prayers of the Church, the Liturgy and the Office, are a great, never-ending rhythm.

Nature, which is a still unspoilt image of God's thought, works through a law of rhythm, a musical law. There is pause and stress, time and beat, there is—and this is the essence of rhythm—a continual gathering to a climax. Actually, this rhythm in nature is a great circle, a passage from birth to death, from death to resurrection. We not only know of it, but we see it, we see morning break and the light gathering to noon and then its slow fading into darkness, and through the darkness to another dawn. We see the green spring gathering colour and fruitfulness and culminating in summer, and after it burns out in a glory of flaming leaves and corn, to seed the earth for another spring.

The rhythm is also evident in our own bodies; we wake refreshed but gather strength with effort, create energy in spending it as day goes on, and in the evening our thoughts close like the petals of flowers and our hands and limbs grow heavy and quiet and God closes our eyes in sleep.

All this considered, it becomes clear why the Church prays through just the same great rhythm passing from birth to death, from death to resurrection. The liturgical year is a year of Christ-rhythm, from his silence in the heart of Mary in Advent, gathering to his passion, from his passion to the darkness of the tomb, from the darkness of the tomb to the daybreak and "lumen Christi" of Easter morning. The Mass itself follows this very same rhythm exactly, and so does each day of the hours of the Office.

From all this it is evident that rhythmic prayer must be pleasing to God, that he has designed everything, to work by a rhythmical law, that we do really fulfill his will in us only when we are in harmony with his great rhythm.

The habit of prayer, already discussed, is the beginning. The idea of night and prayer is a rhythmic idea; short habitual prayers, reiterated at stated hours, are like the stress in music. They have great value in drawing the soul into harmony with nature, of making it, so to speak, work more naturally.

In a flower, God has his unrestricted will; by observing it we are able to guess his will for all that he has made. The flower opens to the sun each morning, each night it closes its petals for the night. But it does not do so voluntarily, no, for it has no will, it is God acting in it.

God wills to act in us in the same unhampered way. In the morning he wishes us to expand to his touch, to open to his light, to "lift up our hearts" as we say at Mass; at night to fold all our thoughts and feelings like the petals of a flower, and absolutely trusting, sleep in his care. He wills to flow through us as life, to be in us as sleep, to utter himself in us.

Rhythm makes the soul as responsive to God's will as the flowers, as ready to open at a touch and shine out with his splendour, or to close and relax into absolute peace.

All day long and all night long, the rhythm of the Church's prayer goes on, and we who are members of the Church share in it. We must do so, because we are all one. Every morning contemplatives praise God, every night they rise and sing to him under the stars, and all day long the rhythm goes on like wave upon wave of love sweeping to his feet.

We ought to be glad that this is so, because Christ is the life of each Christian, we are all one and the prayer of the Church is the single voice of the one Christ in us all, therefore our own voice.

But it is better still for us to increase our awareness of this by deliberately joining in the rhythmic prayer. We can remind ourselves, too, that it is not only uttered on earth but is also on the lips of the saints in heaven and the souls in purgatory. No Catholic is ever alone, no Catholic is ever separated from his fellows, living or dead, and the prayer he wants to join in is not the cry only of one help-less creature, it is the strongest force that there is, stronger than oceans and storms, stronger than armies in battle, stronger than sin and death.

Well, how can we join in it?

Our forefathers did so through the rosary. They could not read and study the Office, so they divided the mys-teries of the rosary to fall in with the hours of the Office. This was good, the rosary has the soothing repetitions of the Office itself and recalls the same mysteries of Christ's eternal love. Those who have time will find the practice very good, and in any case whenever we do say the rosary it gathers in meaning and power when it is said with this intention.

During the reformation, Catholics, scattered and per-secuted, said the Jesus Psalter, that is both a prayer and a meditation in itself, and so simple and rhythmic that it literally sings its own way through the heart to God. For English Catholics it has the glory of having been on the tongues of our martyrs and their comfort in affliction. I know no prayer of the kind which gives such strength and has so miraculous a power to heal the soul and to rock it to the time of God's rhythm, as if it were literally rocked in a cradle of his love.

The Jesus Psalter can be said slowly and go on constantly, taking a day, a week, or a month to complete and, like the rosary, those who can, can say it at the times of the Office if they choose. But the Office is always being said somewhere, so there is no need for too great exactitude.

If all that has been said about relaxing be applied to rhythmic prayer, there can be no greater defence for the mind, it is literally entering into peace. Some people would find it easier to adhere to the idea of one word or one phrase, and if that is to grow from a habit of prayer to the beauty of rhythmic prayer, it must gather until they are saying it mentally all day long, and finally it will happen that the word itself is unnecessary because they are conscious of God and praise him merely by being, and being aware of his life in them. Then each breath is a prayer, each beat of the heart, and the rhythm of the creature flows naturally into that of the Creator—but I am describing heaven.

Perhaps the simplest way is always the closest to heaven, for the effect of rhythmic prayer is so to quieten and ease the heart, that gradually prayer does become just an intense consciousness of God acting in us; we learn at last to realize that waking, eating, loving and sleeping are the supreme prayers, that we pray in so far as we concentrate our whole selves, all our love, into God's will for us, and his will is first of all that we live as human creatures, that we rise and work and eat and love and sleep. Each day is an image of our life, and if we come to pray with each act of each day this rhythm will surely flow into our life, which in the end we shall see simply as one cycle of day and night.

We shall grow through this to saying prayers, above all rhythmic prayer which reiterates through the day, that can begin with one word repeated again and again, and can gather to a full tide of spoken or unspoken prayer, and gradually it will make each moment so saturated with God that as naturally as the flower opens to the light, we shall praise God merely by being what he has made us.

The more the heart is at peace, the more the soul is at rest in God, the more we are free from anxiety, the more God can do his will in us. The flute must be empty to be filled with the breath of God and to utter his song.

The contemplatives do not only chant the Office, they get up in the morning, they work, they eat, they go to sleep at night; and all these things are as much a part of the great prayer as the words they say, because the contemplative is dedicated to God and his life is as close as human life can be to the design of creation.

So we, joining humbly through our beads and our psalters with the whole Church, can join also through our daily life; it is a prayer to rise in the morning, it is a prayer to work, it is a prayer to sleep; when we lie asleep in the act of adoration, God fills us with his life, answering the humblest and loveliest of all our prayers.

From one day, the day from morning until night, we learn our life; it is also ruled by the rhythm which flows from birth to death, from death to resurrection; the soul in the habit of consciously responding to the beat and time and stress and pause of God's will (a habit learnt through deliberate rhythmic prayer) will find that, just as waking in the morning she opens her being to divine love as the flower to the light of the sun, so in the supreme joys of life she will open her whole being to God and her joy will be illuminated by the consciousness of his light penetrating her, his heat and fire of love, making her joy fruitful. And in her sorrows it will be the same, when the darkness comes, be it very great sorrow or death, the soul trained to respond as readily as the flowers to the will of God will quietly fold her thoughts and rest in the eternal Arms until daybreak.

And the daybreak of God! That morning when the tears in the human heart are drawn up to heaven like the dew in the flowers—that is the resurrection, the final culmination of love and joy towards which the rhythm has always been gathering.

FIVE

THE SECOND DEFENCE: AN ATTITUDE TO SUFFERING

Prayer is the first defence of the mind not simply because it is a necessity to the life of the soul, but because it heals the mind and gives it power to think.

This ability to think is essential to the second defence, which is a well-defined attitude to suffering, for this is something which we are bound to think out for ourselves if it is really to be of any use to us, and which We cannot think out unless we are capable of accepting certain knowledge, of making certain observations, of learning certain things at first hand, through experience.

Without the power of thinking our minds are a ready prey to every influence, environment, prejudice or obsession that assails us; and by such things and more we are, now more than ever, assailed on every side.

It is not for ourselves alone that we need to define our attitude to suffering, we have a double duty as Christians: to suffer well and to help others to suffer well. Both these things are impossible if we have not faced the fact of suffering and searched its meaning fearlessly.

Everyone now is bound to have *some* attitude to suffering, though it may be merely an attitude of escape. There is the escape of just not facing it, of clinging to the already too prevalent condition of life-long adolescence; and the widespread regimentation with its striking resemblance to school life, makes this deplorable way not only too easy to achieve but difficult to avoid. Then there are escapes such as taking to drink, which may have been resorted to and which is, after all, only the crudest form of other things accepted by the most genteel, such as constant distraction, continual wireless, a continual facetiousness, on the positive side, and a refusal to read or know the news, an absorption in the pigmy worlds of group, regiment or society on the passive side. All these are escape methods, none are of lasting help to ourselves, all are inevitably aggravating to other people.

For a long time before the war started, thoughtful people discussed suffering as a problem, often preferring the pleasure of never-ending discussion to the responsibility of forming a conclusion, still more often really baffled and unable to arrive at a conclusion.

Suffering is something which challenges us. It happened often in the past that Christians faced this challenge less bravely than others. Too often, while agnostic philosophers faced them, we shut our eyes to such things as poverty, pain or death and fled from the agonies of the spirit.

We have every reason to beat our own breasts and to say our "mea culpa!" But we have some excuse, because the fact that we are Christians makes our responsibility about human suffering so great that it is not altogether unreasonable to want, in our weakness, to avoid it.

The humanitarian who is not a professed Christian feels an obligation to do something to heal, alleviate and prevent suffering; he believes that a day may even come when human effort has made an end of poverty and pain and somehow sweetened the sting of death. It is, he thinks, his responsibility to join in this tremendous effort, to do something, however little, to make mankind happier. But—and here is the key—his responsibility ends with that. He must do something. But the something has a limit. If he fails in his attempt, his attempt has at all events set him free; where he cannot heal, he can pass by, where he cannot end poverty he can forsake it. His duty is to alleviate sorrow, not to share it.

But just where the non-Christian's responsibility ends, that of the Christian begins. He, like the other, has the duty of sharing in the world's effort to break down human misery, but where he fails to heal it he must share it, he can never, with a clean heart, pass it by. That is the essence of Christianity, to follow the teaching of Christ literally, to "bear one another's burdens." The Christian knows that if sorrow comes to an end, the world would come to an end with it. While this world lasts, poverty and pain and death will last too, the torment of the sensitive will go on. And while these things go on, that response of the Christian must go on.

So the challenge of suffering is harder to the Christian than it is to anyone else, and if he has sometimes avoided it, he has much to excuse him; it is, after all, not such a difficult thing to attend a meeting and sit on a committee to abolish men without coats, but it is very hard to take off your own coat and give it to the man without one. And that, on Christ's word, is the way for his followers to face the problem of poverty.

Those few who do face the problem of suffering and respond with a whole will to its uncompromising challenge must, of course, pass far beyond the mere beginning of giving away a coat or a loaf of bread. They must set their pace to the footsteps of a crippled world, and step by step enter into the more delicate sufferings of the mind and spirit. They may not pass by, and the sensitive touch to ease this suffering is learnt only by a lifetime of unfaltering, objective love.

If all this is true in peace time, it is surely not less true in war time. Every day suffering is coming closer and closer to each of us, but it has come already in its cruellest forms to thousands of others and we are faced now, not only with the necessity of forging a weapon to defend our minds from the ravages of our own sorrows, but also to recognize all the world's sorrows as our own. Because we are Christian, we may not shut our eyes. We may not remain passive. We may not take the comfort of wishful thinking.

Suffering is no longer a problem for some, a challenge for others. It is an experience for everyone, the burden of which, if we are Christian at all, we must go out of our way to share.

Do not imagine that I suggest that we Catholics have anything of our own which makes us able to suffer well, or to help others to suffer well, which other people have not. We are not kinder, more tactful, more patient, or more capable than others. We are not better nurses or fire-fighters or ambulance drivers. We are not clearer thinkers or wiser councillors. We should be all these things, for we have the means to be, but alas! We are not!

Yet we have something which even our own unworthiness cannot take away from us, which belongs to even those of us who are the greatest human failures, and which can be given to others only through us. This is the doctrine of suffering, the revelation of God about suffering. It is in this doctrine that hope and meaning and comfort exist, and this is ours. It is the doctrine of suffering which distinguishes Christianity from every other religion, from every other school of thought.

Only Christ taught that it is a good thing to suffer. Other religious founders have taught men austerity, that through it they might at length free themselves from the capacity for suffering. The gentle Gautama Buddha taught thus, and his followers learnt incredible self-denial, but Christ preaches austerity only as a means to an end, the end, love. Man was not to become insensitive, but incomparably more sensitive; he was to suffer because in this world suffering and love have become inseparable, and the Incarnation has no other meaning but love.

This doctrine of Christ is unique. It distinguishes Christianity from everything else, just as our attitude to suffering distinguishes us as Christians. So we have a real trust between us and Our Lord, to know our Catholic doctrine of suffering, to dare to profess it by our lives in the face of the pathetic hedonism of the world, and to be able when, as it will often happen, we are asked to explain it to others.

But our knowledge will be a blunt weapon for the mind's defence, or to offer it to others, if it is not come by through the effort of our own thought. We should have a heart big enough to know what the present suffering of the world looks like to those who have no faith, we cannot bear another's burden if we are incapable of even imagining this despair. We too shall have to wrestle with the angel, as the war goes on; for each of us the war will become our own personal tragedy. We shall not be free of our temptations to doubt, to bitterness, to despair. But we have to-day the opportunity of thinking and learning in order that the defence of the mind, which we bring to this fact of suffering, may be the facing of it with the mind of Christ.

THE PROBLEM

Everyone suffers, young and old, rich and poor, wise and foolish, all without exception. (Or do you know someone who has never suffered?) Imagine a row of empty vessels, ranging from a big pitcher to a thimble. Fill them with water. They are all quite full, but there is more water in the pitcher than in the thimble. So souls can be full of joy or sorrow, brimmed full; but some are filled by very little, some can be filled only by a great deal.

Fill a thimble soul with a slight discomfort and there is no room for anything else. Some people are unhappy to the limit of their capacity because they have a spot on their face, or because a window is rattling. These trifling annoyances exclude all other thoughts, feelings or sympathies. Other people do not seem to be able to concentrate on their own troubles and ailments at all, it requires the world's sorrow to distress them. Above all they are distressed because they do not know how to reach out to them and help. These are big pitchers.

What is the cause of suffering? Some say evil. Others say there is no evil. They say the cause is fear and stupidity and hate, but if there is no evil how can there be fear and stupidity and hate, which are evil things?

People do not suffer through the same causes. Some people commit suicide when they lose their money; others, like Francis of Assisi, can only sing for joy when they have nothing. Some people suffer because they have committed sin, others because they have not. Some cannot see a slum without suffering, others only if they are affected themselves. Is the cause of suffering in ourselves or in our circumstances? What kind of thing makes you suffer most?

Suffering does not have the same effect on everyone. Some people grow big through it; it enlarges them and sweetens them, it fills them with compassion. Others are narrowed and made bitter, personal grievances obsess them, they recall injuries that are years old, self-pity isolates them. Some people are driven by suffering to creative acts, like the great reformers and the saints; others are driven by suffering to destruction or to vengeance; sometimes they destroy others, sometimes themselves.

Is suffering justly proportioned? The innocent suffer as much as the unjust, and what is to be said concerning the suffering of small children? Could a good and just God allow the kind of suffering that is spreading through the world while I write these words? What, if any, is the purpose of suffering, or its use? Can our attitude of mind change the effect of suffering upon us?

Progress is the result of suffering. We learn to walk only when it irks us not to walk; when walking wearies us we invent a car.

The discoveries of science and of medicine are the result of suffering, the struggle to be free and to set others free from limitations and from mental and physical pain. But progress and our use of science and medicine has done so much to paralyse and weaken our natural defences that it is hard to decide whether it has provided us most with wings or with manacles and chains.

Opposites equally devote their lives to the relief of suffering. Some resent it and will not come to terms with it, but cannot rest in a world dyed dark with it; they wrestle as Tobias wrestled with the angel, and their hatred of suffering is their spur to ease it. But there are those who accept it, make more than honourable terms with it, embracing it, who with Teresa of Avila must "suffer or die." They follow the outcast and the afflicted, seeking it, and their love of suffering is their spur to ease it.

It is through suffering that we have all that we have, life and Eternal Life. "We are born in others' pain and perish in our own."

What is it, this thing suffering, which is always different in quantity yet fills every measure; which is of as many different sorts as there are men on earth and yet is always the same thing? Which builds up and breaks down, makes and destroys, sweetens and embitters, which gives death, and gives life. What is it, what is it for?

These are questions which, so far as you can, you must answer, or you must decide to be unanswerable, for you will be asked them over and over again. They are the introduction to the problem of suffering.

THE SCHOOL OF SUFFERING

The world, the ordinary world of everyday, has always been, and is now, the best school of suffering. There is no novitiate so searching, none other where God alone is novice-master and where Christ is learnt so truly. The world is the school in which we can learn the meaning and use and art of suffering, precisely because the world is the school of Jesus Christ—and, as St. Paul would add, of him crucified.

By "the world" I do not mean worldliness. I am not using the words now with the meaning that Christ gave to them when he spoke of the world which hated him and in which he had no part. By that Christ meant worldliness, the harshness of the Pharisees of his time and of all time, the cunning of the hypocrites of his day and ours, the complacency and selfishness of the rich both then and now. Such was, and is, the world in which Christ has no part.

By "the world," as I use the expression here, I mean the environment in which the majority of us now live, in which there is more poverty than wealth, more work than leisure, more injustice than justice. I mean business, trade, labour. I mean the average home, shop, office, workshop, farm. I mean the Labour Exchange, the Poor Relief Office, the hospitals, the Thames Embankment, the docks, the doss houses, the universities. I mean any place you like to think of, where men and women and children come together to assist and to fight one another, to help and to hinder one another in the struggle to live. I mean every condition and circumstance which strikes the heart of man to fire against life, like flint on flint, and so produces the qualities of doctors, scientists, artists, servants, workers, craftsmen, friends, apostles, leaders, lovers, fathers and mothers—and all the rest, who together make up the body of Christ.

This world, then, is the school of suffering. To suffer well, we must have a strong motive. Only neurotics and willfully morbid people find their own vanity a strong enough motive, and those, in fact, seek escape by inventing artificial trials to replace reality. The Christian who finds it necessary to convince himself of his own value by sitting on a pin and eating salt cod is a coward; he has not faced the task of taking his share of the common burden of the pain of sin.

Few people seem to remember that the most powerful thing in the world is the hidden relationship between God and men, that far stronger than propaganda or machine guns is the invisible life of a Christian. One tear, one act of the will that draws the pity of God earthwards, brings peace closer to us than a thousand battles or sermons.

A Christian has this strong motive, of knowing that suffering is creative, need never be wasted. But this motive is made stronger by the fact that no one has the right to consider himself exempt from suffering. No one may think it is unjust that he should suffer. That is because everyone has an absolute obligation to live—not merely to exist, not merely to pickle himself in piety like a gherkin in vinegar awaiting the Eternal Feast. He must live, that is to say, he must recognize himself as part of a whole. He must realize that, as the world's work and suffering are caused by our common debt to God, there is no one exempt from taking his share of the burden. This means that no one may shirk the life, the work, the love of the world.

Naturally, to live implies suffering. To open our hearts freely to our fellow men, to throw open the gates of our spirit, is to invite love, friendship, separation, anxieties, and indeed everything that must mix into its pure gold that alloy we call sorrow.

Pure gold cannot be used for current coin, it is too soft, it must be mixed with alloy. So it is with our life. In this world, the pure gold of life can only stand up to the crude thumbs of the market and buy us the things we live by if it is made strong by sorrow. So, entering life, we accept sorrow—because only through the living of life, through working, through loving, through taking a daily risk of all we have, can we form Christ in us, or share our common Christ-life on earth.

"He who saves his life," says Our Lord, "shall lose it." So it is, those who say: "Why should I suffer?"—audibly, or only by their exclusive attitude—lose their power to make Christ in themselves. They become unable to love, unable to live, unable therefore to suffer fully or well, and so are impotent, unable to help, when times like the present time come, and all who are of Christ are called upon, in the words of the Mass, to "lift up their hearts" and redeem.

First, then, we have the strongest possible motive in that, through the fact that Christ lives in us, our every act has his power with God, therefore our personal suffering has a unique power to help the world, because it always pays off some of the debt for sin, which the whole race is now paying. When we offer him the least hardship or grief in atonement, he must answer by forgiveness and grace.

Another motive is based on the fact that Christ is in other people, that other people are Christ. This is a motive for making our way of suffering one that is helpful to others. Christ in heaven does not suffer any more, he is infinitely happy, and we are greatly mistaken if we imagine that we can do any sort of good to him by sighing before a beautiful carved crucifix or separating ourselves from others to make meditations upon his sorrows. Though such meditations, it is true, are fruitful if they drive us to seek him where he himself says he will be found on earth, needy, hurt and destitute in the men, women and children of the world.

This motive affects both our willingness to discipline ourselves in order to be able to help and our whole attitude to other people's sufferings. There are many people who have been brought up in "sheltered" homes, where they have been kept away from the sight of sickness, of the grosser manifestations of sin, and of death, where in fact they have been prevented from coming to Christ in his passion. It is through work, through mingling with all sorts of people, through taking our share in every-thing, that we come into contact with human suffering in natural, unforced ways. So, the Christian who wishes to atone, to bear his share of the burden, to heal the wound festering at the world's heart, will learn the way, not by regarding himself as an exception, but by beginning with humility to look for the blessed things of life, but with a willingness to pay for them and the certainty that he will suffer through them.

We can choose what kind of suffering we will have—whether it will be big, redeeming, reaching out to others, or whether it will be small and sterile. If we choose to live an exclusive life, to narrow our souls in a timid state of selfish soul-culture, we will certainly suffer. We will suffer bitterly if we are forced to sit in a draught, if we have a slight cold, if we hear a door slamming. We will suffer particularly if there is a demand made upon us to give of ourselves, if we are threatened by the loss of one jot of that precious life we are so intent in saving in pickle for eternity, and our suffering—though ever increasing, out of all proportion to the cause—will be absolutely fruitless.

On the other hand, if we choose to take on ourselves the necessary austerity for training ourselves to be able to live lives that contribute to the world's good; if we choose to respond and say "yes" to everyone who wakes in us the spark that may burn to love, to say "yes" to every experience that may make us understand human creatures better, our suffering will be big and our capacity will grow big enough to include that divine thing, compassion, which word does literally mean sharing in the passion.

At present, under war conditions, there are literally thousands of young women who might never have seen crude suffering at first hand, let alone have lifted their own hands to tend it, but who are now in the hospital wards, learning not only to be useful at a time when usefulness is a way of being human, but also learning to recognize Christ, as Veronica did, not in the ivory crucifix, but in the blood and sweat and tears of helpless humanity.

The power of compassion, of entering into and sharing the passion, does not end in the immediate surroundings. It is true that what you do to the nearest at hand is done to Christ, but it reaches Christ far off too. Through the great mystery of the oneness of all Christians you cannot do anything which does not affect them all.

The air raid warden who faithfully gets up at three o'clock in the morning and keeps his cold vigil in the streets is actually lending a supporting arm to the far-off Christ in Finland, who is marching through the snow. The V.A.D. doing up the broken hand of the workman who meets with a slight accident on her monotonous post does in fact bind up the wounds of Christ, bleeding in Poland. More still, with every brave acceptance of suffering of any sort, the Christian infuses more love, more courage, more grace, more Christ-life, into all Christians. It is true of all energy that it is increased only by spending; this is as true of the Christ-life as of all else. In proportion to its spending it is increased in the human heart and in the whole world.

The upshot of these motives is that suffering well involves a whole attitude to life and a whole way of living. It is not something which can be practised for one hour a day, or can be tabulated, counted or organized. It involves the strong motive of love and all that that inevitably leads to.

Our lessons in suffering well will take a practical course, first finding our motives, learning the true value of the thing, and then the practise of the discipline and austerity we call training, learning to make our desires active. In the services for home defence, the opportunities are unrivalled, we have to learn to obey, to be independent, to face ugly sights, to do without sleep, to rise at all hours, day or night; and all of that has this great use, it sets us free of egotistical suffering and sets our sail for the vaster sea of Christ's passion. That is the value of bodily discipline; when you have learnt to suffer the cold without being obsessed by the cold, you have reached out your hand to the lonely prison camps of Siberia. Such austerities free us of self, they sharpen the perceptions of the soul and they teach us to know Our Lord personally, in himself and in others. They are the door opening into the kingdom of compassion. We need not seek them, it is enough to accept the conditions of service and to realize what they can really mean.

Paul Claudel, in one of his superb poems on the Stations of the Cross, says: "There is no cross found among

us that his body will not fit; There is never a sin in us, but
some wound answers it."

Now if with the eyes of our mind we contemplate the
crucified Christ and look at his wounds, we discover how
true that is. Men use their hands to kill. Christ nails his
still to die. Men grasp for riches, for the pride of life, honour and soft clothing. Christ is naked and shamed before
everyone. Men seek escape in drunkenness and the mis-
use of the senses. Christ thirsts and his eyes are blinded by
death, his ears are filled with mockery.

Now if this is so, it must also happen that in the mystical Christ, the Christ still crucified in us all, there are
also wounds to answer the particular sins of our age. Our
reparation will consist in accepting these wounds. One
in particular—boredom. It seems odd to speak of boredom in the same breath as the great agonies that are now
being endured, but the fact is, boredom is an intense suffering, and one of which the young complain every day.
But it is not only the young who do—hush! Don't say a
word, there are the most high-sounding sighs from ascet-
ics soughing across the ages, in which the intolerable
boredom is described as "aridity of the spirit," which it is!

At the present time boredom has assumed huge pro-
portions. It has become a problem—but what has brought
the world to its present pass? Or at all events contributed
to it very much? Emotionalism; not, believe me, strong
emotions, but the cheap sensationalism of weak emotions which, being rooted in no faith, seek restlessly and
endlessly for more and more ready-made satisfaction.

Everything for years has contributed to it; the books on the market, the pictures, the cinema, the conversation, the penny press, and the whole vibrating atmosphere of hysteria which must arise from the sum total of it. Is it surprising, therefore, that one of the wounds inflicted upon the mystical body of Christ is boredom—aridity?

What can answer this sin so well as the emptiness, the dryness, of the real aridity? It is not only the wretched A.R.P. worker, stifling her yawns at the First Aid Post, who is atoning through boredom; it is all who have somehow lost their zest for prayer, who seem to be emptied out like old husks, who think they are failing because they are not feeling. So, whilst strong, vibrant emotions rooted in God are good and very good, boredom is also good and is one of the wounds answering sin. We may be dry husks, but the scattered grain is the bread of life, and it is sown.

Another besetting sin is want of shame, a callousness to wrong, which is not recognized as evil and is even exalted. Answering this, is the condition which has come to be known as the "guilt complex." The only complexity about guilt is the fact that it is not the guilty but the innocent who are most humiliated by the sense of it. God knows, there is tragedy enough through the wrong sense of guilt, but there is surely a vocation also to feel guilty for all those who are guilty and don't feel it.

And so it goes on and on; out of the chaos and confusion of modern life the contemplative eye will gradually discern wound after wound on the mystical body of Christ, pleading with God.

Why has this school of suffering grown so in the world, so that it seems to fill the world? This is why. Fear, hate, pride, have grown and grown and are spreading through the world in the form of destruction, cruelty, death. No arms can win the victory over these forces, only one Force can oppose it, that is the force of love; this force of love is generated by every Christ-act, by every accepted suffering, by every prayer of every Christian. The most humble invalid who can do nothing else but sit in her room at home with folded hands shares the splendour of the martyrs whom we know give their lives daily now; they, the martyrs, share their grace with us, and we by this inexhaustible miracle of Christ's life in us, support them by our small sorrows.

Surely these thoughts answer Our Lord's question: "Ought not Christ to suffer these things and so enter into his glory?"

How can we, "other Christs" as we are, not welcome those lessons in the school of suffering, which bring us into his glory, in our fellow-Christians and in heaven? It is because we are "other Christs" that we ought to suffer these things.

But this glory? What is this glory into which the poor little shivering air raid warden, with his red nose and his blue fingers, is now entering? It is the glory of the risen Christ. If he had not risen we could well despair; "but as it is, we can be sure that all and everything, great and small, that we have to suffer is a sowing of seed, and that after this winter a spring of Christ will come; even in the human race, there will be a time of his flower and fruit, the summer time of his love, peace that is based upon a simpler and holier living and is won by the passion. A wounded race we shall be, but how blessed the wounds, when the stigmata of divine Love burns on the risen hands and feet and heart of the race that his sorrow has saved.

WHY SHOULD I LEARN?

We never do anything well if we are not convinced that it is a good, reasonable thing to do. If it is something that involves a difficult technique, we require a very strong motive to attempt it, otherwise we may start eagerly, but when we find out what great courage and patience are required of us we shall throw the thing up.

You may well ask if it is a reasonable thing to *learn to suffer well.* Would it not be much more reasonable to learn how to avoid suffering, as indeed so many try to do? Why say that there is a meaning in suffering, a "use" in it, and that it is an art? In the answer to these questions the first lesson in suffering well is hidden.

To try to avoid suffering is useless, for the seed of it is in the human heart. There is a child being brought up at present by a group of people who think that they have created conditions which will save that creature from all suffering; they are trying to keep it out of her life, by keeping her in secluded luxury and surrounded by joyous, beautiful ideas and so on, but the seed of sorrow is in the child's heart. A similar attempt was made six hundred years before the birth of Christ, when the little prince Gautama Buddha was brought up in just the same way, but before he was thirty years of age his heart, broken by the world's grief, drove him to seek peace in forsaking, not the sorrows of life, but the joys of it!

If it is useless to avoid, or to try to avoid, suffering, if suffer we must, it seems at least as reasonable to do it well as it is to speak well or to walk or sleep well.

That is the lowest reason. One note higher in the scale is this: suffering is caused by sin, we have all some sin in us, we have all committed sins and do commit them, and so it is just that we pay the price, and in doing so we do something for our own salvation.

A note higher still: suffering is, because of sin, the common burden of humanity. By taking our share of the burden with a will we lighten it for everyone. But many will dispute that. "Think of the Finns," one will say when another shivers in England, and the poor shiverer answers, not without reason, "I shall not make them warmer by being cold myself." Everyone must suffer, and everyone must be affected by suffering. It will either make people bitter and hard and perhaps mean-spirited and always on the defensive, or else it will make them sympathetic, tender and pitiful and understanding, with a readiness, even a longing, to throw off their defences in the service of those who need them. The effect of suffering on the individual will depend on his attitude to suffering. Those who see it as a just thing will not be bitter. Those who even taste God's mercy in it will be enlarged. But those who resent it will naturally be embittered.

On the purely natural plane, what we are either makes life happier or more unhappy; a bitter, gloomy person makes everyone he meets less happy, he can make his own family life a real hell on earth. A person who is full of understanding and who consequently judges others kindly not only makes everyone he meets happier, but over and over again helps to rebuild a broken life. Therefore the way one suffers must make the world either sadder or happier, one or the other it must do. By suffering badly I add to the common burden, by suffering well I lighten it, and that only on the natural plane.

The scale ascends now and we strike lovelier notes. My personal suffering can lighten the world's sorrow, by redeeming the world's sin. If you are baptized you are a Christ, to be "christened" does literally mean that, to be Christened. Because we are each of us a Christ, our sorrows are his passion continuing in the world.

If Christ had come down from the cross as the Jews begged him to, he would not simply have become the greatest of all failures, he would have gone away from our hearts which are nailed in grief. But remaining, he remained in us. In our turn we have to be glad to remain on the cross for others as well as for ourselves.

I come to the point now which is perhaps for most people the greatest incentive of all: namely, the really great power that our suffering has to help the world. Far greater than the effect that one who suffers well has on his fellows is the effect on God.

You could say with some excuse that God may well turn from man and leave him to his misery. We have his promise that he will treat us as we treat one another. Look around the world and see with what incredible cruelty men are capable of treating each other.

Sentimentalists are continually saying that God is love and so could not allow anyone to perish in hell, that God is love and so could not allow evil to triumph on earth. Might it not be as logical to say that God, Who is love indeed, will turn away from and abandon men who burn, drown, suffocate and torture each other? Who do these things, not only in cold blood, but after years of deliberate preparation, who use every resource of nature and science and all the might of the human intellect to wreck the lives and break the hearts of one another? Is it so unreasonable to ask, could a God who is all love take these people to his heart?

This is the answer: In men God sees his only Son. He does not see us so much wicked as hurt; it is not so much our sins he sees as the wounds sin has made on the body of Christ.

God cannot resist Christ. Sin it was that crucified Christ, and when he was on the cross, God did not curse the world because he was suffering there; instead he forgave it. Do you think this strange? There was his only Child, so tortured, made so ugly with grief, "Having no comeliness whereby we should know him"—might not God have cursed the world?

He did not, because the last light in the darkening eyes of Christ pleaded for men. Every wound on his body bled for men, all that he had was taken, he was naked and homeless that men should be clothed and have homes. With his last breath he prayed for men, and with the last beat of his heart he loved men. So when God looked at him, he did not see the wounds as we do, because he saw them glorified by love, and God, Who is himself Love, cannot resist that.

As we are "other Christs," God also sees us in that way, and the more we have encouraged the Christ life in ourselves, the more redeeming our sorrows are. Therefore suffering is the most powerful of all prayers. It keeps the passion of his only Son before God's eyes, and keeps the dying of Christ before him as our one true plea for mercy. No father can refuse his dying son, and God is the Father of Whom the most loving earthly fathers are but caricatures.

It is true that we do not see results. If my tooth aches and I take it well and offer it in love to God, I shall not see a slum dwelling dwindle and flicker out like a spent candle and in its place an ideal home sprout-up like a flower bursting from the bud. But the result happens, more grace, more courage, more hope on earth, and because the debt has been paid in the only coin God can take, there is in fact alleviation of sorrow.

There is yet a further motive. To suffer gladly when we must for the love of men is indeed not only the closest imitation of Christ, it is the essence of our own Christhood; but when Christ is formed in us (as he certainly is when we have learnt that much about suffering) we shall have a desire to adore God. This is bound to be so, because our minds will be like Christ's mind. We shall desire to be grateful, to respond for every good thing, every flower or star, every moment spent happily, we shall want to thank someone, we shall want to be conscious of the presence of One Whom we can love without measure, in Whom we can delight without fear of loss, in Whom ultimately our griefs will be lost as a flame is lost in the light of the sun—in a word, we shall want to adore. This is certain, for Christ's intellect was concentrated wholly on adoration of his Father; therefore he did not only pray, he made himself a sacrifice, the most complete adoration; the sacrifice of the cross.

This we also can do through our suffering. Adoration—were it widespread on earth—would not only use, as it were, this great burden of grief that is everywhere, it would lift it and put it on the plane of joy, for it would gradually draw every heart to the light of God, making us conscious of him in everything, and in him there is our only lasting joy.

Here, then, are reasons *to learn to suffer well,* natural and supernatural. We increase human happiness by allowing suffering to enrich our natures, we grow in understanding, pity, and natural love; we pay our share for the debt of sin; we grow in Christhood and have the power of Christ to move God. We keep Christ's passion ever before God's eyes, and finally, with the very heart and mind of Christ, we adore God.

OTHERS IN THE SCHOOL

I used to give a coin to a beggar every evening. I passed him going home from my office, and I was glad that when I passed him it was growing dark; the merciful twilight helped me to avert my eyes from him. I could not face the man's misery. His face was disfigured, by disease it seemed, and his eyes were eyes into which I dared not look.

One day I read about Saint Francis and the leper: how the debonair young man passed the leper with horror, flinging him a golden coin, then suddenly he turned back, wounded as it were by grace; he threw himself down from his horse and embraced the poor man. That was the beginning of the most lovely, the most lyrical sanctity the world has ever known. From then onwards Francis became poor, he became homeless and he began to sing; he attended lepers from then on until he died, and on his own body he bore Christ's wounds.

What had happened? Francis had seen Christ in the leper, and from then on he became Christ's contemplative in all poor men, in all broken lives. He saw Christ in them all, and because he recognized Christ he could not content himself by giving him money and distant pity, he had to become like him, he had to suffer with him and he had to serve him in his suffering.

People say that what we look at for a long time, what we live with, we come to resemble. There seems to be a truth in it; people's dogs, for example, become like their owners, and that not only in face but in disposition; it is instructive to spend an afternoon at the window noticing the resemblance between the passers-by and their dogs.

From continually looking at and living with Christ in humiliated men, from contemplating him through the ugly and filthy wounds inflicted on him by sin, Francis began to reflect his beauty. Those wounds began to be shadowed in the saint's own body, and one day they broke out in points of burning light. Francis was blind, he could not see God's glory shining on his face, he could but feel the pain and joy of it in his soul and his body.

The world has been glad enough to fling Christ Our Lord a coin in the gutter and pass on with eyes averted. We have not dared to face him. Suffering has been hidden. Hospitals, prisons, workhouses, doss houses, walls round pain and grief and death, even our customs and conventions have joined in the conspiracy, it had become bad taste to show when we suffer.

If we heard that a friend was bereaved we felt shy about offering sympathy. We were afraid to probe such a wound, and made our clumsiness an excuse for silence. We were afraid of, and embarrassed by, other people's suffering, and even by other people's sympathy.

Now war has come, and it is no longer possible to keep pain shut away like something shameful. The time has come when we must face the sight and touch of suffering. We can hope for one great good, as we are bound now to face these realities and to try to train ourselves to do something about them. We may succeed so well that when war is over we can dare and even desire to go on, to go into our prisons, to find not only the bodily, but also the spiritually maimed and to serve them, to go into what remains of our slums and to insist that it remain no more. We can let our training be not only for war but for all of our life. For we can learn Christ not from only the gospels, but from every single person with whom we come in contact. Moreover, we learn both with the heart and the head or not at all. I go further. I learn with the heart, head, flesh and blood and all five senses, or not at all. We learn, as Thomas the doubter learnt at Christ's command, by touching his wounds with our hands, or we miss him and do not know him at all.

Christ is in everyone with whom we come in contact. In our employer, our secretary, our office boy, in our grocer and plumber, in the policeman who takes the number of our car, in our cook and in our bishop, in our husband, wife and child, in our friend, in our lover, in our pet aversion. You can think of anyone you like; in that person Christ is, and is there to be known and loved and served in this world.

If we are not interested in the minds, the feelings, the hopes, fears, sorrows and joys of everyone with whom we come into contact, we are not interested in Christ. Whatever we do to anyone, we do to him. If we are impatient with the mental suffering, the doubting, questioning and wrestling with the angel, of more sensitive minds, then we are impatient with the mind of Christ bleeding under the crown of thorns. If we shrink from the broken lives of sinners then we draw away from Christ fallen and crushed under his cross. If we will not go to the sick and the afflicted and the poor to help them, we will not help Christ.

How shall we educate ourselves to face other peoples' sufferings? First, on the physical plane. We can now go into the hospitals and work for the sick. Those who are doing it will find that this work, which outside of a picturebook is monotonous and hard, will come to life if they learn, like Francis of Assisi, to see the wounds of Christ in each one: They must not think of a ward full of "cancers" or of "decrepits," they must not think of people as "casualties," "cases" and "operations," but as Christs. They can think of him in the hospital as being helpless, just like he was in the manger, and when bound up again in the swaddling bonds he was carried to the grave.

Outside of hospitals, outside of national service, there is the great harvest of the forgotten poor. In our zeal for our country we have forgotten that if we do not work to keep the little homes and loves and lives of our people, our victory would mean nothing. We are not fighting for might, but to keep those conditions in which the love of Christ can still bear a flower that lifts an innocent face to

God from this earth; if we forget our poor now we might as well surrender at once to those who tread the Christ-bloom of the world into the mud.

So, every Catholic who is not fully occupied could still learn to help suffering by going to the local Sister of Mercy, and through her meeting poor people whom he or she can help, and he or she can begin her education by sweeping and dusting the homes of the poor, by learning to take charge of the children and to cook a meal.

But there is another, more general way of teaching oneself to face up to the world's suffering. Instead of for-getting, remember. Remember that everywhere people are in need, and you have to face this need. You can begin at once by learning to do without that others may have more. As a child I used to rage when I was told that a good motive for eating up all my disgusting rice pudding was that lots of poor little girls who were starving would like it! That struck me as a very good reason for giving it to them. I have not changed this view, but I add to it now that I ought to learn even to feel a little hungry, to give up some dishes I do like, to the poor little girls who are starv-ing. The same applies to clothes, to amusements, to ciga-rettes, to everything now; if we can train ourselves to be ready to give up and do without, we shall have something to give to Christ in his need and shall even get the habit of giving. There is no one who could not find one per-son poorer than himself and to whom he could constant-ly give something; this is the very best way to learn to be mortified, and being mortified is essential if we are to face other people's suffering.

But the suffering of Christ in men is not confined to the physical plane. In the first place, bodily suffering itself is inseparable from mental suffering; they go together and act and react on each other, and moreover, there is a rapidly rising tide of mental pain. For every thousand women who can now dress a wound on the flesh, there is only one—if as many—who can begin the healing of a wound in the mind. Mental wounds, wounds of the spirit, like wounds on the body, tend to become poisonous; and like bodily wounds, they will do so if those who attend to them infect them themselves. It requires much more education to attend to a broken heart than it does to attend to a broken leg.

How are we, in our school of suffering, to study this? First of all, we can do it by very carefully and very continually observing other people. If we regard such things as bitterness, temper, rudeness, defensiveness, as symptoms of pain we shall be right. We will find out over and over again that if only this person can be brought to reveal his unhappiness his nastiness will heal up.

We can study human nature from everyone we meet. We can read books which are written by people with long knowledge and experience, and we can make an honest, almost scientific, study of our own failings in a spirit of charity to ourselves and others! For example, I think A would like to bite me. Now, have I ever bitten anyone? Why yes, I bit my sister when I was six! If I remember rightly, I was not even a very bad-tempered child. As it happens, I thought she was going to bite me! Now is it possible that A thinks I am going to bite her? Or that her attitude to life is that everyone is going to bite her? May it be that life has, in fact, been hard to her, always, or at some very sensitive point? There is no doubt that this way of studying human nature will help one to face human suffering and to know what to do.

One good result of the war is that in the war services social barriers break down. That is to say, that whilst nature insists that the various types, trades, strata of people still tend to form into groups, the barriers separating these groups as human beings break down. In the services, all types of people meet, live and work together for a cause dearer than life to them all. This gives a very great opportunity for people to know and study one another more. It would be a very big advance in the school of suffering if the same spirit of equality as human creatures not merely were encouraged everywhere but were defended and preserved after the war. How often in the past people have said that they want to help the poor, the sick, the spiritually ill, but that they do not know how or where to begin. Now, war has at least made it all too easy to begin, and here is the practical summing up of what is here suggested, simply by way of educating ourselves to be able to face and to help those who suffer. We can learn to nurse and tend sickness and wounds, actually in the hospitals; we can lift this work from horror and drudgery by seeing Christ in each patient.

We can learn to tend and cure sickness and to care for old people, over-worked people and little children, in the homes of the poor. We can learn to know something about the causes and the cure of mental suffering, by observing people, by talking to all sorts of people, by being honest with ourselves, and by reading.

We can fit ourselves for endurance by self-denial, by accepting the rigours of national service in the spirit of love, as a deeper preparation to serve, by adding to this such generosity that we shall always have something to give. We can make all this more alive by actually giving what we give up to Christ in some person. But above all this, the beginning and end of it indeed, we shall educate ourselves to dare to face suffering if we do, literally, take person after person as a Christ and so contemplate him until at last his wounds reflect gloriously on us as they did on Francis, though maybe at that time we shall not be able to see ourselves.

Suppose we do in fact learn these lessons well, what an incredibly lovely thing it would be if we heard Our Lord saying one day: "You were always preoccupied with Me! You gave hours and hours every week to studying Me, your deep interest in Me made you endlessly patient with Me, you did not wait for Me to be wounded, you applied yourself to months and months of tedious study and practice that if I was wounded you should be ready; you set yourself free by self-denial for My sake, thus you were free of the burden of your body. In this way you could give up sleep, you could be cold and hungry for Me. And above all you perceived My loneliness, the loneliness of My mind, and you crowned yourself with thorns, learning to understand Me."

THE MYSTERY

To the Christian, suffering is not a problem to be explored by the human mind, but a mystery to be experienced by the human heart. A mystery, the catechism tells us, is "a truth which is above reason, but revealed by Jesus Christ."

Christ's revelation about suffering is woven all through the gospels. Sometimes his words are puzzling, as if he wants us to ponder them and discover our grain of truth through a certain effort; growing in the effort, expanding our souls for the joy that they are going to receive. "Ask," he says, "and you shall receive, seek and you shall find, knock and it shall be opened to you."

At first sight there is much to puzzle. Suffering, he says, is a blessed thing. Blessed to be poor, to mourn, to be reviled and persecuted. He even warns those who enjoy the opposite. "Woe to you rich—woe to those who laugh now"—and so on.

Suffering, or at all events our willingness to risk it, is the one condition he makes for his friendship. Never once did he ask of those who wanted to join the motley little company of his friends if they were virtuous, sober, honest and respectable; never once did he attempt to persuade or charm anyone to his service with fair promises of happiness. On the contrary, with uncompromising honesty he said: "If any man will come after Me let him take up his cross daily." "And whosoever doth not carry his cross and come after Me, cannot be My disciple."

You might suppose that, longing for love as he did long for love, he would at least have encouraged those who ran to him with ardent enthusiasm; but no, to the young man who said, "I will follow Thee whithersoever Thou goest," he answered in the loneliest words that any man has ever uttered, "The foxes have holes and the birds of the air their nests, but the Son of man has nowhere to lay his head." As if to say, if you want to come with me, you must live my life, and my life is a life of sorrow, of homeless, wandering sorrow.

This warning of Christ was no mere test, it was not like the traditional trial of love in the fairy stories, something that would evaporate as soon as the right answer was given: no, of those who accepted his challenge one died by his own hand in despair, all the others were put to death, saving one only, the most loved and most loving, John, who lived on and on for nearly a hundred years and suffered the more terrible martyrdom of not being able to lay down his life for Christ, of living out the years of loneliness without the sight of the divine Face that once his eyes had seen, without the closeness of the human Heart on which he had once laid his head.

Yet Christ, Who had made this demand of his friends, was always trying to alleviate suffering. He could not bear to see the widow woman weeping for her dead son, so he gave the boy back to her alive. He was always healing, forgiving, going about doing good to everyone. He wept openly when he saw Mary Magdalene weeping for her dead brother, although he knew what he would do, knew that in a few moments she would be overjoyed. He broke down at the sight of a merely passing grief.

But there is no occasion when Christ called into his own fellowship one whom he had cured of blindness, lameness, sickness or death.

What a number of contradictions is raised in all this! Christ bids everyone to try and ease suffering. He does so himself. It seems that he can hardly endure the sight of it, yet he offers it as the only inducement to his friends and he says that it is blessed. Later, the same contradiction is visible in his passion. At the beginning he says that the hour has come in which he will be glorified, yet he shrinks from it and even asks to be let off! And when he has endured everything, all temptation, the sight and sense of all sin and guilt, the injustice of the condemnation, the betrayal by his friend, the stripping of his garments, the hour in which he was forsaken by God, he comes to the disciples on the road to Emmaus and asks them this astonishing question: "Ought not Christ to suffer these things and so enter into his glory?"

What can it all mean? What is the meaning of suffering?

Suffering is the result of sin; poverty, pain, sickness, death and all the torments of the mind, all are the result of sin.

When Christ was born, the world was already full of suffering. He did not bring the cross into the world, it was there already. The cross was a dead weight, it was the result of sin, and it punished sin, it offered no hope. Suffering was not a punishment planned, so to speak, by God. "God desires not the death of a sinner." God loved the world, but man had made for himself the misery which was his punishment.

When Christ became man, he uplifted man's nature together with all its vital activities. He changed man's suffering into his passion. Man's suffering became redemptive.

By himself, no man can atone for sin, not all the united suffering of the world could atone for one small venial sin, because sin is against God, and so only God can atone for sin. But because Christ is God and he has given his own life to be man's life, man's sorrow has become Christ's sorrow and everything is reversed.

Now the cross, which was a dead weight, bears flower! The world's tears, which were cold and sterile, are changed to strong life-giving wine, like the water of Cana. And now, one small suffering of the most insignificant human creature can atone for sin.

When Christ's earthly life ended and he ascended into heaven, he did not remove his life from man. He left himself on earth, in the sacred Host, and in the heart of man.

Man's sorrows continued to be Christ's sorrows, Christ's passion. They continue to atone for sin. All the suffering we see today, all the suffering we know in our own lives, is the passion of Christ. If Christ had not changed our suffering to his passion, we should still have suffered, but suffering would have been futile, destructive and useless.

Christ was not content simply to redeem us. He did more, he became one with us. He took our lives and made them his life. There is only one explanation possible—love. Love asks and wants union, it wants nothing else. Real love can stop at nothing else, it desires not only to share in the life of the loved one, but to live it, not to be with the other, but to be the other. If anyone denies this, the answer is simple; he has never loved.

The whole meaning of our Catholic faith is union, union with Christ, and through him, union with one another. This oneness is not a unity of ideas or ambitions or acts or circumstances, it is not a unity such as one finds in a society or group, it is an organic wholeness. It is oneness like the oneness of the various parts of the human body. Because this is so, no Christian can be separated from any other Christian by anything whatever, we are one with our dead, we are one with our distant martyrs, we are one with our sinners.

This oneness gives our suffering an added value. It means that whatever of good one Christian does, all Christians share. So, we can act for one another; if one Christian sins, another can be holy for him, if one Christian dies for his faith all those who tremble share in his glory. And any Christian child in the schoolroom can go into the white snows of Siberia and give courage to the heroic bishops there.

Because all men's sorrows are Christ's sorrows, we can always find Christ on earth. "If you did it to the least of these little ones, you did it to me." The healing and service given to each other is given to Christ, we can clothe him and feed him and amuse him and love him in each other. What we refuse to each other, we refuse to Christ. We may not know it, but every stir of pity, of compassion, of generosity, of tenderness, is the fruit of the passion.

As Christ grows in the Christian soul, and as she comes to see with his vision, it is in others that she sees him, for she is looking out, not in, and as he did, she has compassion on the multitude. She sees them with all the marks and effects of sin covering them, but in them the innocent Christ, needing her help. In the hospitals, she sees him helpless in swaddling bands. In the refugees and the Poles and the Finns flying from their ruined cities and homes, she sees him flying from Herod in the desert: In the dying she sees him upon the cross.

This, then, is the essence of Catholic teaching about suffering. It is man's punishment, made by man, but changed by Christ to his redeeming sorrow. Through Christ, suffering has become, not an evil to be avoided at all costs, but a thing to be accepted willingly, even joyfully, as a means of sharing in the redemption of the world.

CONTEMPLATION THROUGH
SUFFERING

There is a way of contemplation through suffering. Christ taught us this way from the cross. It is a bridge of love across which God comes to man and man goes to God.

To practise it is this—you look at Christ until you become like him, just as by looking at the sun you become golden like the sun. You touch his wounds, and from them you learn the measure of his love. You share the experience of his passion with him, until through loving with his love you become one with him.

The risen Christ said: "Do not touch me!" He has a mysterious life of illimitable joy, secret to everyone but his heavenly Father. But, paradoxically, he told us to touch his wounds. "See My hands and feet, that it is I Myself: handle and see." It means this—

We cannot see Christ in his glory, but we can see him and touch him in man's suffering.

Our contemplation in the world is the contemplation of the humiliated Christ in mankind.

Humanity is the veil of Veronica. It is, so to speak, the suffering Face of Christ on the Via Crucis, impressed upon man, his face covered in blood and sweat and tears, just as we do literally see so many human faces now. This disfigurement is caused by sin, exactly as Christ's historical passion was caused by sin, so is his passion in us. It is he Whom we meet every day and in every house and every street, and were it not that his love has transformed even the wounding and bruising of sin, we should meet the ugliness of despair everywhere. As it is, Christ, by giving himself to our humanity as he gave the impression of his Face to the veil of Veronica, has given his own mysterious beauty and significance to every tear on man's face, to every drop of blood shed from his veins.

So it is Christ Whom we look on to-day, in the casualty posts, in the hospitals, in the shelters, in the streets. We see him in the wounded, in the helpless old people and the infants, in the bereaved, in the homeless, in refugees. We see him as Veronica saw him on the road to Calvary. In the helpless we see him in the swaddling bands and burial bands and in the Host. In the outcasts, as he has been through all the years and is now, an outcast from his own kingdom, the human heart.

Gradually, through looking at Christ in these suffering people, we begin to have some faint idea of the measure of his love. The extremes of it are no longer hidden. He is stripped of his garments. Those garments, under which we have tried to conceal the fierce, disquieting passion of his love, are torn off—convention, respectability, security. He is stripped of all this in men, the excess of his love is laid bare.

God does not change, he is "the same to-day, yesterday and for ever." Christ on earth chose to be more homeless than the wild fox and the birds, to have nowhere to lay his head; today he is still destitute in the destitute, homeless in the homeless. He chose to be dumb and helpless in his mother's womb, in the borrowed tomb, in the host, and to-day he remains inarticulate and helpless in the helpless and dependent who, in the swaddling bands of infancy or old age, lie dependent on others in what borrowed shelters they may. There is no expression of his love, no part of him that does not go on in the world now, because we are his body on earth, and he cannot be broken up, he must be in us whole; and he is.

We cannot begin to understand this without wanting to respond to such love and to comfort Christ in all mankind. His everywhereness and everyoneness is a drag at the heart. The whole human race is one with him, not merely the people of London, of England, but all people everywhere. The wonder of this stirs the mind that is not utterly dead, with new sacrificial life, as the hidden green shoots stir the dark earth with new springs. We want to reach out to him all over the world, in Poland, Finland, Holland, Siberia, France—and, yes, in Germany. But we are too small, we cannot even reach those who live in our own town, or only a very few of them; indeed, there is only one person who can answer this tremendous challenge of Christ suffering in man, that is Christ himself.

We have got to stretch Christ in us, then, to fit the size of this war, the cross overshadowing the whole world, just as the soldiers stretched him to fit the size of his wooden cross. The arms of Christ stretched on the cross are the widest reach there is, the only one that encircles the whole world.

Christ must grow in each of us to the size of his passion in us all. "Without Me you can do nothing."

Looking at Christ in man, we see that there are very many "unconscious Christs"; people who, through the grace of the Church, share his life and passion without knowing it. It was told of a boy with no conscious religion who, refusing to forsake a wounded comrade in France, and having no means or skill to help him, sat by him at the risk of his own life while he bled to death in a field. This boy had a revelation that night; suddenly he knew life to be not the round of girls and of amusements that he had thought it, but the life-blood of a man, and instinctively he thought of Christ on the cross. It seemed to him that in this dying of his young friend, which only that morning he would have cried on as useless waste, there was splendour and purpose far deeper and wider than any obvious motive of patriotism; all the grief and terror and loneliness of that night was changed to wonder and faith. He did not know why, it was the faith of a blind man who knows more through his sensitive fingertips than many who have the light of their eyes, it was the faith of the man whose child was healed: "I believe, help Thou my unbelief."

But it is obvious, he was *in fact* present at the crucifixion, and he was there because he was taking part himself in a Christ-done deed, even though he did not know it. The revelation that he had came to him as it came to the good thief and to that other soldier, the centurion on Calvary, through *seeing* the extreme of love.

Many of us would like to give our lives like that young soldier, but the question arises, how can someone who hardly knows Christ really die a Christ-death?

The answer is in the fact of our oneness in him. St. Paul described it, and his imagery must have been repeated thousands of times; he uses the image of the body, and says that one part cannot say to another: "I have no need of you."

Humanity is indeed the living body of Christ. Each part is essential, not only for the well-being of the whole, but for its work. An artist carving is using his hands and head; you cannot say that he could do it without his hands, and certainly his hands could not without his brain. You cannot say that a man's fingers think, yet in a sense they seem to, so sensitive are they, so immediate in their response to his will. The oneness of the body is a miraculous oneness. It is the same blood that floods the brain with life and flows through the heart and the unbelievably sensitive nerves, so that a man's will seems to tingle in his finger-tips.

Did the carver cut off the tip of his little finger at his work, it might very likely happen that his will would bleed white and he would die; the life does not depend on his little finger, but all the same his little finger seals it in his body.

Christ is in his body on earth like the life in that carver; and he is here in us to do his work, and his work is love. If his integrity, his wholeness, compels him to remain in his hunger and thirst, in his wounds and his weariness, in his childhood, his manhood, his birth and death, if it causes him to stay with us as a teacher, a friend, a brother, a servant, a child, it must also compel his *will* to remain in us, and some human beings belonging to his body on earth *are* Christ's will on earth. It may well be that to these the opportunity of literally dying the soldier's death will not come, but because they are one with the redemptive Christ, and because they are the Christ-will, they are on every battle-field, united to everyone who dies there, driving the Christ-life to them as the blood to the finger-tips, carrying his purpose of love to be consummated in them, as the nerves in the body that make mind and heart and hand and eye one thing.

On the cross, Christ was man's contemplative. He looked upon man and loved him, and he did indeed become like him, indeed his whole body, covered from head to foot with wounds, showed the world plainly what man is like: "he had no comeliness whereby we should know him." But it was not only before men that he was thus; before God he had all the sins of the world on him, so wholly had he identified himself with what he loved.

But Christ could not touch man's suffering or even his shame, without changing it, as he changed the colourless, tasteless water at Cana to strong red wine; he lifted sorrow on the cross, lifted it to the level of sacrifice, and sacrifice is adoration.

For man, adoration is necessary; rob him of the awareness of God and he will adore anything that assumes mystery, because it is bigger than he is. He will adore a big machine, or the idea of a relentless state. It is adoring false gods that has brought the world into war.

The contemplative, who sees Christ in man, who touches his wounds, who loves with his love, keeps Christ's will-to-adore alive in the world, keeps bright and pure his will-to-sacrifice, speeds the blood-stream of his life through the whole world, gives the intrinsic value of his love to every generous, blind act men do.

To love with his love, that is indeed the purpose of such contemplation. To be Christ's will, to love God with his love and to love men with his love, it means doing what he did, dying to self. Christ went to the limit. He had to; he is love, and love must be complete. He loved to the end, that is, to the extreme length, the limit. The limit of Christ contemplating man was death: the complete humiliation of death.

There was never darkness like the darkness in the dead eyes of the Light of the World; never deafness like the deafness in the ears of the Son of man when his head lay on his mother's heart and he no longer heard it beating; never dumbness like the dumbness of the Word of God when Christ was dead. But never was mankind more fitly crowned than when the bowed head of Christ was tormented with thorns. At that moment it was not only himself that he lifted up, but everyone.

The first step on this bridge of contemplation is looking at Christ in man; the second is touching his wounds and believing; the third is identification with him, becoming one with him, loving with his heart.

It means this; from wishing to turn away from suffering, we shall wish to face it; from fearing to approach others in sorrow we shall come close; from the isolation of an egoistic prayer our hearts will expand and open like roses opening in the darkness, to the splendour of adoration.

The contemplative in the world, the nerve-cell carrying blood to the finger-tips, will never be alone, will never be left to his own loneliness even for a second, because there are always the hidden men and women who are the contemplatives in the cloister, who have mastered the art of dying daily, who are the very heart of the body of Christ and pump the life-blood into every limb. Just as we are one with distant soldiers, distant prisoners, countless people far away, the cloistered contemplatives are one with us, doing the same work. The fire-watcher sitting in the dark by his bucket of sand, his axe at his waist, watching, can think that other men, too, are keeping his watch, are speaking to God and saying what his inarticulate heart would say for him.—All night, all day, contemplation goes on; all night, all day, Christ's heart at the heart of the world, with us to suffer and to redeem.— "And lo! I will be with you always, even to the consummation of the world."

SIX

THE RISEN CHRIST

On the eve of Good Friday, when the Office of the Tenebrae is gathering to its midnight, when the pre-sanctified Host lies as if in the tomb, at the very moment when we would expect the heavy curtains of mourning to be drawn closer, there is a sudden breaking of light. Flames and flowers throng the Altar of Repose, a mysterious joy possesses the children of God. In the deepening twilight of her sorrow the Church rejoices because inevitably Christ must rise; from the hearts of her countless children the Christ-seed must break into flower. The grave that holds the body of the Lord is deeper and wider than the cave hewn in the rock, it is as deep and wide as human nature, it is Man.

At Christmas Christ is born in us, he takes the littleness of our nature to himself, his innocence is given to us. The Christ-child grows to manhood; the simplicity of our daily life, working, eating, drinking and sleeping are woven with his glory.

On Good Friday he lays hold of the cross with the hands of a lover, takes to his heart all that dire misery, ugliness, brutality, that is the result of sin; even that he transforms. Suddenly, the age-long sorrow, death, becomes potent with life. The seed has fallen into the earth, the great emptiness of the world's heart is filled with the potency of immortal love.

Easter is Christ risen in us; from now until the feast of the Annunciation our life is the risen Christ. Christ will flower in us, will bear fruit in us, will come to harvest in us.

Had he not risen in the flesh, but remained in the tomb, he would have been the prerogative of the devout few. In every age the Magdalenes and the Johns of the world would have come with their precious ointment of love, but the Christian world would have been a world of weeping. Because Christ is risen it is a world of joy; an unassailable kingdom of heaven in the midst of surrounding sorrow.

It is for the ordinary man, the creature of flesh and blood, that Christ has risen; for those who cannot look upon folded hands and still feet and listen to the silence of a heart no longer beating.

We know now in what way he would live in our humanity. Not as One who, having proved his love, has gone back to his Father leaving us a sealed tomb, but as

One who, having tasted to the full the joys and sorrows of human nature, having embraced the grief of mankind, having drained death to the last bitter dregs, sets his wounded feet in the dust again, takes bread into his wounded hands again, and seizing a doubting friend's hand, thrusts it into his wounded heart; as though saying by his every act to all who would ever tremble and doubt: "I did not wipe the tears from the face of sorrow to lay sorrow by. I did not touch pain with a fierce redeeming beauty to have done with it; I cannot give Myself into the arms of death to cast death aside! I made all these things My own that the glory I gave to them should be yours, that whilst they remain with you, I shall remain with them." He has taken all those things to himself, and has changed them all for us.

Sorrow has not ceased to be sorrow, but it is no longer simply a punishment, it is something with its power of healing in itself, something that redeems, something that makes joy possible to men.

Christ experienced the bitterness of sorrow, living our life, that we might experience its splendour, living his.

"Had he not risen," says the great St. Paul, "our preaching is in vain." The ordinary man can say no more; were it not that he is risen, our Christ-life were impossible.

Had he laid aside his wounds with his life, then we must have known even Christ comes to the limit of love and ends it. But it is not so, having taken the weakness of our nature, he has made it our strength. Now, if we set out to bear one another's burdens, we know that however heavy they are, however hard to us, Christ has already borne them, and bears them now in us.

"Until your hands are folded," he says to each of us, "My hands shall lift them, to work, to tend, to heal; until your feet are still, Mine shall make their journeys; until your heart is for ever at peace in Mine, Mine shall beat in yours." He must remain in all living men. That is the uncompromising demand of his love; he will not remain like an ikon enshrined in the rare meditative mind, but will live in the warm-living men and women of flesh and blood, who lead the common life and shoulder the burden of living.

He must go into all the workshops and offices, down all the mines, work in the fields, gather into earthly barns. He must walk all the streets of all the cities of the world, die on all the world's battlefields, dwell under the eaves of all the world's homes. He must be in the workhouse, the prison, the hospital, he must be with men and women, with boys and girls, with the child in arms.

Easter then is truly the resurrection of the children of God, because they are to live his life, the life that has overcome sorrow and death. There is no longer anything in life that can defeat the joy of the human heart, not even sin, for sin it is that wounds the world as the nails wounded Christ. And when the sharpest grief of all wounds a man—sorrow for sin—the evil thing falls away as the ugliness and torment of death fell away from Christ; but the wound remains as his wounds remained when, alone with his Father in that secret daybreak of Easter, he lifted his hands as they had been lifted upon the cross, and God saw the Light of the world in five stars, two that shone from Christ's feet in the dust, two that shone from his hands in supplication, one that burnt from the heart of the risen world.

DISCOVERING THE RISEN CHRIST—IN OTHERS

At first sight it is faintly disconcerting that none of his intimate friends knew Christ when he appeared to them risen!

But perhaps the risen life recorded in the gospel is meant to show us not only how Christ lives in men now, but also how we can discover him in one another; if that is so, the mystery is explained.

A great many people pride themselves on the exclusiveness of their circle of friends, they catalogue people; "the people who count," "those who are safe," "nicepeople!" and "people who are useful." Within this circle they live virtuously, but they are terrified to step outside; their virtue, or themselves, is too precious or too fragile to be submitted to the handling of the common world of men. In extreme cases such people end up by thinking that they are poached eggs in constant danger of falling off the toast, every lunatic asylum has its poached egg; in the less extreme cases they are not certified and they are often honoured, but they never discover the risen Christ.

Why? Because they do not want to discover him where he is in ordinary men and women, in all sorts and conditions of people, even those who don't count—are not safe, useful or nice.

The first condition of discovering Christ is a burning desire to do so; we know by faith that he is in men, this alone leads some people eagerly into all sorts of human contacts, seeking something more than the exterior, seeking, wanting to discover Christ. This desire, when it is strong enough, has two results; those who have it simply will not give up hope of finding him, and their courage gathers in proportion to their love.

Mary Magdalene, mistaking him for the gardener, said, "If only you will tell me where his dead body is, I will take it away"—preposterous! How could she, a woman, take it away? And what an exaggerated, peculiar and useless thing to do. But Christ reveals himself with a word, her name spoken with such grateful love that now she knows him.

Those who never despair, who are eager to take to their hearts even those who seem dead in sin, that, warmed by their own Christ-life, Christ may rise again, are certain to discover him. Those who do not fear, or who conquer the fear of the crudity of people and life, who go to the most needy with compassion like myrrh in the hands of Mary, must discover him in men. So there is desire, the will to recognize that this ordinary dull person, that peculiar one, this one who is unknown, is a Christ or a potential Christ. Then courage comes, to take risks, to face realities, to form contacts, and the disinterestedness that makes one a fool in the world's eyes.

Peter, in spite of all the glory and sorrow of the past years and the tragedy of the last days, went back with dogged pluck to his old job—"I go a-fishing—" There is no better way of forming contacts with people than work. Those who work with the majority and believe in the goodness and wisdom of their fellowmen, those who in difficulty and grief have the kind of humility which, instead of closing up like an oyster, is open to receive comfort, kindness and advice from others—these too, like Peter with his breaking net, must discover Christ risen.

On the road to Emmaus the two disciples were heavy and broken because they did not know where Christ was. They had pinned their faith on his teaching and they realized that without his presence on earth it would be impossible to follow it. Gradually, through the gathering warmth in their minds as they listened to the words of the Stranger who joined them, they began to guess . . . when he broke the bread, they knew; they discovered the risen Christ. Every one of those who saw him had to discover his identity through some human gesture. They all mistook him for an ordinary man. Mary speaks, as she thinks, to the gardener. He calls her by name, she knows him. Peter sees a man making a little fire on the seashore; it is a Christ-like gesture, suddenly John knows: "It is the Lord."

Those who are open to receive his kindness from others will know him. Equally those whose hearts are hospitable, who entertain others, who welcome strangers, who are glad to share what they have There is an old saying: "Hospes venit—Christus venit."

All those who discovered that the Stranger was the risen Christ, had this in common, in their desire for him they ceased to be self-conscious, forgot themselves. Peter's shame did not stop him in the tomb, Magdalene's notorious past did not even make her hesitate to question the gardener.

No one will recognize the risen Christ who is concentrated on self. Christ will be there, but those who wait to be saints before they greet him will certainly miss him.

To Mary, a word was enough. But Christ, who above all wanted us to know he was really flesh and blood, knew and used an unfailing way of convincing men. He ate with them, then they believed. He insisted on his realness, his needs, his wounds, on being touched, on eating with his friends.

Is it not clear that those who do literally the works of mercy in the catechism will discover him, those who don't will not? Touch the wounds of mankind, supply his needs, give him food, that is Christ's meaning. Those will discover Christ risen in men, who keep the two great commandments, who bear one another's burdens, through doing the work of the average worker, through having a broad heart to everyone, through forgetting self, learning to reverence the positive glory of the common humanity in which Christ lives his risen life.

In Ourselves

If we have discovered the risen Christ in others, there is yet more joy for us. One day we will discover him in ourselves. If we are poor we shall learn to choose instinctively the inward joys, to select; in a life not crowded by material things we shall discover the lasting beauties, the poetry, the thoughts, the recreating things that depend not on money but on perception. Poverty that seemed drab will begin to fill with a radiance like the grey sky filling with dawn—we are selecting with Christ's values. Or fear may come—something to be faced, a responsibility, before which we crumble—then the strength of Christ will flow up through us and flood our hearts; we are facing it with Christ's courage. Or we shall face sin, stark and brutal, in another, and we shall suffer with a compassion that is too big to condemn, and be certain that God would not give this kind of pity in vain—we are redeeming with Christ's sorrow.

Even in the extreme thing—our own sin—the unlimited mercy goes on. Now he is absent, now he is dead in us; we know *now* what we had before and took for granted. We are sorry, and the colour flows back into the bloodless Christ, the seed stirs in our hearts again, it breaks out into a flowering of love we had not dreamed of before.

He is risen in us, and now what do we keep of the sin? The wounds, the wounds with which he has redeemed all sinners, the sorrow which we are glad to have for a seal upon us, that we may put our hands into God's Hands again.

As we grow, that joy in those wounds upon us grows, for we understand that all the wounds in the world are the wounds of the risen Christ, and so when we lift our hands to God and show him the Hands of his Son, we can say truly: "Father, here we are at Your feet, all Your children, all the world, for You have but one Son in Your sons, and through his resurrection I am Your Christ."

THE RISEN CHRIST—IN THE NATIONS

If this war is the passion, then it is quite certain that Christ must rise again in the nations as well as in individuals. Men and women whose faith is no more than a wistful longing to be able to believe in *something,* are convinced that a new world must come after the war; they feel instinctively that it will be a better world: Everything will be renewed, a new understanding between nations, a new social order, and all for the better.

It does not seem to occur to those who believe so ardently in what we all want to believe, that there is a law of cause and effect; the natural result of nations bleeding themselves white in order to destroy each other is not understanding, and better social conditions, it is, on the contrary, bitterness, poverty, disillusionment and despair.

There is no more pitiful illusion, none so likely to bring us to yet worse tragedies, than this: that men must be kinder, wiser, more just, because of the war; that the comradeship of common endurance must go on in peace time; that everyone will cling to the asceticism forced on him now, for the sake of justice, when the war is over.

After the last war, we heard this slogan everywhere: "Make England a country fit for heroes to live in!" We did, alas!, so well that among large numbers of the community it was not fit for any but heroes to live in.

The sorrow of this war will not end with the fighting, it will outlast the natural lifetime of any of us who are living now. Nevertheless, Christ will rise again.

My faith is his rising is based on only one thing, that this war is the passion and the passion is the sowing of Christ's seed, the seed that the earth may not deny.

During the past years we have come to know other countries through their sorrows; from being fantastic, far-away places to most English people, they have become real. They have gradually appeared through the mists, and we have seen that they are not stranger countries, but Christ-countries. We know them because we know the Crucifix, and they are crucified.

In country after country the same thing has happened; out of the fog of politics, of folly and cruelty, Christ has emerged. In thousands of men and women and children in Russia, Mexico, Spain, Czechoslovakia, Hungary, Austria, Germany—and now in Poland, Finland, Holland, Belgium, France, Italy, Greece, Romania, England.

The only unity that exists now between these countries—and it does exist—is the greatest unity of all, the only one that could bridge across the injuries and bitterness of this war, the organic oneness of Christ in his members. In them all, he will rise again. That rising cannot be organized, it cannot be seized upon by human societies and crystallized into a fixed plan to be imposed upon everybody, it won't show itself in material things, or in a worldly triumph for religious bodies, or a kind of mass revivalism—it will very likely be as secret as it is now, and more so. For Christ does not change. It was when he was lifted up on the cross and crowned with thorns that everyone saw him. When he rose from the dead, even his apostles were slow to believe it; of the few who saw him none at first knew him.

His rising in the men and women of the nations cannot differ from that first Easter. It cannot be, as so many still seem to expect, a repudiation of himself, of his way. It cannot be the kingdom of God changed to a material kingdom, a triumphant, prosperous, comfortable civilization based on Christianity; that is impossible. Had Christ ever consented to that he would have let the legions of angels come to his defence two thousand years ago: he did not. He does not now, he never will; for his kingdom is in the human heart, it *is* the integrity of the human heart.

Even after he rose from the dead, Christ went away and his apostles saw him no more, and he told them why; because if he did not go, the Paraclete would not come. The Paraclete, the Holy Spirit, was to bring him closer, he would be not only with them, but in them.

The Paraclete teaches all wisdom, gives vision and strength, comforts and renews; we can pray for the coming of the Paraclete, because we know that Christ's passion in us all must be the prelude to that pentecost.

The Paraclete cannot give us any new teaching, but can only bring home to us Christ's wisdom; but in that wisdom will be the world's blessedness. It can teach us to hold fast to those lessons of simplicity and love that war has taught us, and enlighten us more. It can help us to remember that we are part of a whole; knowing that is true humility. The only greatness we have is being part of the body of Christ, and learning from him meekness and humility.

The Paraclete comforts in the midst of sorrow; makes strong; and teaches that there is joy in the poverty which denies self, yet more that no one may be destitute, that there is joy in working with hands and head together, that snobbery, the pride of life, the desire of money, and the lust for power, destroy all human happiness; that the flesh is holy, and in holding it in reverence is our own and one another's peace; that the beating of the human heart is a miracle of wonder, life a thing to cherish, life itself, we must not kill and we must love, and the simplest human love, be it consecrated to God, is holy. We are the bread of the sacrament of life. We genuflect at the words: "Incarnatus est" in the creed, for these words mean Christ abides in our flesh and blood, in our humanity.

Many "other Christs," civilians and soldiers, have died; before the war ends many more will die; long before peace is declared those dead will be united, pleading with the Paraclete to come to us, for these dead are all one in Christ. Just one host lifted for the world, be they English, Polish, German or French, and they have gone away for the reason Christ went, that the Paraclete may come.

True enough, many could not have formulated that intention, but all, though it may be blindly and not seeing how it could come about, died and will die in the hope that their death would somehow bring man's happiness closer. And so it will, simply because the war is Christ's passion, and therefore the sowing of his seed.

Therefore, the unbroken, undivided Christ must rise, and between all nations the torrent of his life must flow; and where politicians can fail and statesmen blunder, the people, the multitude, who have suffered, cannot.

Secretly, in the hearts of those who set the wounded feet of Christ in the dust again, who lift up his hands again, showing their red stars to God, wisdom must come, Christ's seed must break; not seen by the world, there will be a oneness between nations and classes, the beginning of a revolution of love, a unity, that will not be imposed on men from above, but will begin inside like a seed, and grow.

We can pray with trust for the descent of the Dove, for the return of the Paraclete, for him to come back, the warm Wisdom God, as the bird comes back from the sun to the very tree and the very nest she had last year, and if she finds it rifled builds it again in the same place.

Our living and dying is a prayer for this, for wisdom to know "the things that are to our peace." And Christ has already answered—"The Paraclete, the Holy Ghost, Whom the Father will send in My name, he will teach you all things and bring all things to your mind, whatsoever I shall have said to you."

CARYLL HOUSELANDER (1901–1954) was a lay English artist who became one of the most popular Catholic spiritual writers of modern times. Though a woodcarver and art therapist for children, her true gift was sharing a unique and mystical vision of Christianity and Catholic teachings through her writing.

A Spiritual Classic
by Caryll Houselander

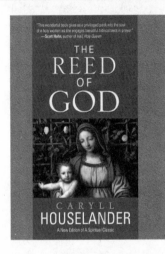

Reed of God

First published over half a century ago, Caryll Houselander's *The Reed of God* is a spiritual classic that deserves to be rediscovered by a whole new generation of readers. Houselander's beautiful and profound meditation depicts the intimately human side of Mary, Mother of God, as an empty reed waiting for God's music to be played through her. Houselander shares her insightful and beautiful vision of Mary on earth, Mary among us, Mary as a confused but trusting teenager whose holiness flowered with her eternal "Yes."

ISBN: 9780870612404 / 192 pages / $11.95

This wonderful book gives us a privileged peek into the soul of a holy woman as she engages beautiful biblical texts in prayer. In ways witty and winsome, Houselander teaches us to unite our will with God's will, as the Blessed Virgin Mary did.

Scott Hahn
Author of *Hail, Holy Queen*

ave maria press®

Available from your bookstore or from
ave maria press / Notre Dame, IN 46556
www.avemariapress.com / Ph: 800-282-1865
A Ministry of the Indiana Province of Holy Cross

KEYCODE: FD9120700000